The Essence & Teachings of
Bhagavad Gita

Blessings from Mother Saraswati

Radha and Lord Krishna

The Essence & Teachings of *Bhagavad Gita*

Rajiv Sachdev
Neeraj Gupta

STERLING PAPERBACKS
An imprint of
Sterling Publishers (P) Ltd.
Regd. Office: A-59, Okhla Industrial Area, Phase-II,
New Delhi-110020. CIN: U22110PB1964PTC002569
Tel: 26387070, 26386209; Fax: 91-11-26383788
E-mail: mail@sterlingpublishers.com
www.sterlingpublishers.com

The Essence and Teachings of Bhagavad Gita
© 2014, Rajiv Sachdev and Neeraj Gupta
ISBN 978 81 207 8982 1

All rights are reserved.
No part of this publication may be reproduced, stored in a retrieval system or transmitted, in any form or by any means, mechanical, photocopying, recording or otherwise, without prior written permission of the author.

Printed in India
Printed and Published by Sterling Publishers Pvt. Ltd.,
New Delhi-110020.

Dedication

This book is written in the loving memory of my Parents

Foreword

The Bhagavad Gita is one of the most widely circulated spiritual texts in the world, directed not towards any particular community, caste or country, but to humanity at large. Its teachings are universal and can help to spiritually guide genuine seekers regardless of which path they are following.

Down the ages, from Adi Shanakara to Sri Aurobindo, great commentaries have been written on the Gita which, along with the Upanishads and the Brahm Sutras provide the three foundations of Vedanta. Thousands of other books have also been written based on the Gita and its teachings in all the languages of the world.

In the present attempt, Rajiv Sachdev and Neeraj Gupta have chosen a few select verses from the Gita and presented them in an attractive manner. I am sure the book will be useful to spiritual seekers, wherever they may be, and I wish them well in their endeavors.

Dr. Karan Singh
Member of Parliament (Rajya Sabha)

CHAIRMAN
Committee on Provision of Computer
(Equipment to Members of Rajya Sabha)

Preface

This book is about a life journey. The life's journey did not start with this birth and is not going to end with death. It continues. It has been there for an undefined period—more than age of the Sun, Moon and Earth. We have always existed in some form or the other and we are always going to be there. Hence, comes up the curiosity of where we were and where we are going to be. Well no one knows—some people do know, they are enlightened souls, they exist among us but they keep quiet and share it only with some pure souls dedicated to Lord. For others, the knowledge in scriptures is the guide.

This book is based on *Srimad Bhagavad Gita* and on Hindu Scriptures. *Bhagavad Gita* is one rare scripture of Hinduism that got narrated by God so it has the messages for the humans with no interpreter in between. While the book is based on Hinduism, this book is widely read by people from all religions. Finally all of us terminate with the same God. We all draw energy from the same God. We are all children of the same God. We have seen Him in different forms at different times. But He always existed with us. He is as near as inside us and that is where the enlightened souls have met Him. He is so far that we will never reach Him if we are not pure and if we are not turning our journey in His direction.

Where does the need come up for reading scriptures when people are intelligent and logical enough to decide what is right and what is not. Yes, there is a need; we are intelligent on the material journey, how to earn more, how to live better, how to make life more comfortable, how to do charity as we have more and how to respect views of learned and elders. All this knowledge is clouded with material attraction and pride.

Scriptures are scriptures, once you follow them you will discover how different your understanding of the rules of life was. That is what happened to Arjun. *Bhagavad Gita* was narrated by Lord Krishna to Arjuna and we today have the blessings to follow God's teachings.

Bhagavad Gita was narrated over 5000 years ago in India in the battlefield of Kurukshetra. A Scripture revealed in the battlefield! Arjuna was an enlightened soul. He had won over sleep which means that he did not need sleep, and he actually did not sleep during the war that lasted for 18 days. Winning over sleep cannot happen with determination. Determination is there in many people on this earth but can they decide not to sleep? It happens with purity and blessing from the Goddess who monitors sleep. Arjuna with his physical body could ascend to Heaven and he brought many weapons for war from the Heaven. We do not see people having that level of God's blessings today that they can ascend to higher worlds with their physical body. Such God's blessings come only to purified souls advancing on a journey towards God's home. To such a soul, Lord Krishna questioned his knowledge about the rules of life and what one should do and what one should not do. God said that your knowledge and wisdom is clouded. If such a soul could be guided, we can understand that there is a much deeper need for guidance for all of us.

We all stand in different levels of material richness depending on our financial status, our country of living, family wealth, inheritance, blessings. We all also know that this journey with our current body is going to end—there are no exceptions, not seen, not heard. With this awareness, we do have a curiosity about what is going to happen and that is exactly what this book is about—on what is going to happen based on knowledge in the *Bhagavad Gita*?

If you start your journey towards south, you will reach south. If you start your journey towards east, you will reach east. This is simple to understand as science is going to help us determine the direction and we can go in that direction and we know what we are heading towards.

Scriptures guide you on the same thing—journey—where are we heading after the journey of the soul in this body is completed. We are not finished. Are we going to go to God's home, or are we going to Heavenly worlds, or are we going to be human beings again, and if yes then born as Intelligent people in pious families or born as an unfortunate child in a starved environment, or even lesser is the lives of lower worlds like species in water, insects, animals. These are all governed by God and we are advancing our journey in one of these directions. This is serious; we need to know our destination and *Bhagavad Gita* enlightens us with the rules of the journey which are in brief explained in this book.

I revealed this immortal Yoga to Vivasvan (Sun-god); Vivasvan conveyed it to Manu (his son); and Manu imparted it to (his son) Iksvaku. Thus transmitted in succession from father to son, Arjuna, this Yoga remained known to the Rajarsis (royal sages). Through long lapse of time, this Yoga got lost to the world. The same ancient Yoga, which is the supreme secret, has this day been imparted to you by me, because you are My devotee and friend.

— Lord Krishna

Bhagavad Gita, Chapter 4, Verses 1-3

Lord said that this Yoga got lost to the world so it means that what was revealed by Lord through *Bhagavad Gita* had gone missing from the world.

Lord says it is a supreme secret. This is a supreme secret as it explains God's home and also guides on the journey that a worthy one can embark on to reach His home. This remains a secret as it gets known only to the deserving ones. Lord says that this has been imparted to you by me, because you are My devotee and friend. This knowledge will be understood only by pious devotees.

The very fact that *Bhagavad Gita* was revealed in the middle of the battlefield inspired Arjuna to perform his natural duty and fight an unsolicited religious war for the sake of suffering people and eradicate the error from earth. Performing all your natural duties forms a key message from Lord and how this natural duty is to be performed so that it becomes eternal and leads one to God's home is a hidden supreme secret in *Bhagavad Gita's* messages from the Lord.

Rajiv Sachdev & Neeraj Gupta

Contents

	Foreword	6
	Preface	7
1.	Lord Krishna	13
2.	Battle of Mahabharata	21
3.	Mother Radha – Soul and Consort of Lord Krishna	28
4.	Yogamaya – Sister of Lord Krishna	37
5.	Blessings by Birth	45
6.	Four Destination – After This journey	54

- Three Gunas for Three Destinations
- Heaven Away from God's Home

7.	Meera Bai Pure Devotional Love – Prema Bhakti	73
8.	Faith in Him	83
9.	Bhaktidevi Tulasi Maharani	88
10.	Journey of a God-realised Soul	94

- Sattva Life
- Sacrifice
- Meditation
- Renunciation and Dispassion

11.	When the Journey Continues	123
12.	Complete Surrender	131

'Discarding the injunctions of the scriptures, he who acts in an arbitrary way according to his own sweet will, such a person neither attains occult powers, nor the supreme goal, nor even happiness. Therefore, the scripture alone is your guide in determining what should be done and what should not be done. Knowing this, you ought to perform only such action as is ordained by the scriptures'

— **Lord Krishna**

Bhagavad Gita, Chapter 16 Verses 23 & 24

Lord Krishna

Bhagavad Gita was revealed by Lord Krishna in the middle of the battlefield more than 5000 years ago. It is important to know about Lord Krishna, the battle of Mahabharata and important heroes who engaged in this war and the circumstances that led to this war.

Lord Krishna is an incarnation of God or God Himself on earth. Prabhupad ji, says Lord Krishna is 'Supreme Personality of Godhead'.

Lord Krishna was born to Vasudeva and mother Devaki in a prison. They were imprisoned by mother Devaki's brother as he learnt that the eighth child born to his sister will be the one who will kill him. He jailed his sister and his brother-in-law. He killed the first six children. The seventh child was transferred from Devaki's womb to Rohini's womb by Yogamaya (Lord Krishna's sister). The seventh child is known as Lord Balarama.

Lord Krishna was born as the eighth child to mother Devaki but at the time of the birth, Vasudeva exchanged the child with the daughter of Nand and Yashoda (Yogamaya—Lord Krishna's sister and divine potency). This secret was known only to Vasudeva and Nand as they had planned to change the child. A daughter was born to Nand and Yashoda on the same night as arranged by Lord Krishna. The daughter was no other than the form of Goddess Durga in the form of Yogamaya—the internal power of Lord Krishna.

Devaki's brother, Kansa, was told that a daughter was born and when he tried to kill that baby girl, she flew to the sky and appeared as a Goddess with many hands. The Goddess told Kansa from the sky that the eighth child of Devaki and Vasudeva was already born and he would be killed by the same child.

Lord Krishna

Lord Krishna was born in Mathura. Mathura is about 200 kilometers from New Delhi. He was born around 5200 years ago. He was son of Devaki and Vasudeva but Lord Krishna was brought up by Nand and Yashoda. So Lord Krishna is worshipped as son of Devaki and Vasudeva and is also worshipped as son of Nand and Yashoda.

Krishna was taken to a distant place in the middle of the night as the Lord was born at midnight which is celebrated as Krishna Janamashtami. The place where Lord was taken is known as *84 khamba*, the house that has 84 pillars. Vasudeva took baby Krishna hidden in a fruit basket. This place is also near Mathura and a highly blessed pilgrimage space today.

Lord spent first 7 years of His childhood in this house which was the house of Yashoda and Nand. Baba Nand was the king of that village and believed to have owned 125,000 cows. Lord Krishna's home had plenty of everything as He was son of a king. When Kansa learnt from the Goddess that the child is already born, he ordered few demons to kill the new-born children all over Mathura.

Putana was a lady demon who reached Lord Krishna's place and tried to kill Him. She was killed by Krishna when Lord Krishna was just few days old so Lord used His supernatural yogic powers in this incarnation. In the first 7 years of His childhood, he playfully got rid of most of the demons from that place so no one realized how all those killings happened.

Lord Krishna loved cows. He along with His friends also used to steal butter from the houses in the village. In those days women used to prepare butter from milk and there was abundance of milk and butter in every home. This group of children wandered around, sneaked into a house and broke the milk pots where butter was kept and enjoyed eating the butter.

Over the period, this news spread in the whole village and complaints started coming to Mother Yashoda every day who failed to understand as to why her child would steal butter when there was enough of it in His own home; but the stealing and mischief did not stop.

The ladies started hanging the pots of butter from the ceiling to save the butter from this group of mischievous children, but soon the children started making a pyramid and stood one over the other and reached the ceiling. Krishna used to be on the top and he would break the pot with His flute that He always carried with Him. One day when they formed the pyramid and Krishna was on the top, suddenly the lady of the house came back and everyone ran away. The pyramid broke and she found Krishna hanging with on to the pot on the ceiling as all the children below Him disappeared. She took Him to Yashoda with butter all over His face to prove that Krishna was the one who planned with other children and stole the butter. But Krishna proved His innocence again that he had been falsely implicated.

There are hundreds of stories about Krishna stealing the butter and proving His innocence to His mother who always believed Him. The ladies of the house enjoyed Krishna stealing the butter and then finding an opportunity to complain against Him, so much so that when he did not steal the butter, they used to encourage Him to do so, so that they could catch Him and complain against Him. It was sort of an enjoyable game to catch Him and complain against Him.

Some ladies then hung bells around the butter pots so that when children attacked the pots, they would come to know. This became a hindrance in their stealing activities as the group got caught more often than they used to. So Krishna made an agreement with the bells that the bells would not ring when the children stole the butter. The bells agreed dutifully. Next time when the group was stealing the butter, the bells did not ring so all children had a good time eating the butter. As soon as Lord Krishna put the butter in His mouth, all the bells started ringing so He alone was caught as the others ran away. Later Lord Krishna asked the bells as to why they broke the agreement. The bells replied that Duty came first. When the Lord eats the offering, it is their duty to ring so they were quiet when others ate but had to ring when the Lord ate. Duty is above all agreements. Today, in all Hindu temples bells are rung when an offering is made to Gods.

Tired of listening to mischief and complaints, once Krishna's mother had to actually tie Him up so that he stayed away from making trouble. That day Krishna broke the pot of milk right in front of her eyes at home. Not only that, He fed the butter to monkeys and children and created a mess in the whole house. Now mother decided to teach Krishna a lesson. She ran after Him with a stick and finally caught Him while Krishna was trying to get away.

She could not tie Him even after trying for a long time as the rope was not long enough. But that day she was determined that she would not leave Him. Children were shouting and requesting His mother to leave Krishna. Krishna was also holding His ears and pleading but mother had decided that she would tie Him down this time, no matter what happened.

Lord Krishna was also struggling hard to escape His mother's hands but He saw the determination in her eyes and understood that there was no getting away that day. Finally, He gave up and let His mother tie Him; there is a saying that He can be tied by one who is determined to tie Him with love.

He was tied to a pillar and he tried to move out from the house and dragged the pillar with Him. As He moved out unnoticed by His mother, the Pillar got struck between two huge trees and when He tried to pull the pillar, both the trees fell down. They were two high souls from the Higher Worlds who had been cursed to be born as trees, and they were instantly absolved of the curse with the touch from Lord Krishna.

The day when this happened is the same day when Deepavali is celebrated and when Lord Rama returned to His Kingdom. Devotees celebrate the whole month as *Damodar* month (which is *Kartik* Month in Hindi Calendar and comes around October/November) and offer Ghee Lamps to Lord Krishna and Mother Yashoda every day.

It is also believed that mother Yashoda was not the first one to tie Him, before that once mother Radha had tied Lord Krishna with a Golden belt for not keeping His promises and it did not happen on earth but in Lord's abode above Time. Radha could tie Him because of her immense Love for Him.

When Lord Krishna was around 7-8 year old, they left Gokul where he spent His childhood and moved to Vrindavan. Vrindavan is named after the name of Vrinda. Vrinda is *Tulsi* (the Basil Plant). Tulsi is worshipped in every Hindu home. We will read about Tulsi's story later in this book.

Once Lord Krishna ate clay like most children normally do at a certain young age. Mother saw Him eating the soil and asked Him to open His mouth. When he opened the mouth, Yashoda saw the whole universe in His mouth. She saw Earth, Sun, Moon and all the planets in it and she was puzzled. This incident happened when he was less than five years old.

When Lord Krishna was around 8 years old and they had moved to Vrindavan, He advised worshipping of Govardhan Mountain. God Indra got upset with this decision and his anger resulted in continuous rain and thunderstorms for 8 days which would have drowned the village but Lord Krishna lifted the mountain with His one finger and gave shelter to all the villagers and their cows. It is after this that God Indra realized that Krishna (Supreme Lord) had taken birth on earth and he named Lord Krishna as Indra of Cows as He loved and saved cows. Hence He came to be known as 'Govind'.

Govardhan Mountain is worshipped by Hindu devotees.

Krishna killed Kansa (His mother's brother) at the age of 12 as was ordained by the Goddess. The Goddess had told Kansa from the sky that the eighth child of Devaki and Vasudeva will kill him. Lord Krishna spent His childhood in Gokul and Vrindavan. Then he moved to Mathura and later to Dwarka.

When the battle of Mahabharata was fought, it is believed that Lord Krishna was 80 years old. By that time, He had killed many demons and bad kings who had been cruel to their countrymen.

During the battle of Mahabharata, Lord Krishna did not use any weapon himself. He drove Arjuna's chariot. It is on the first day of Mahabharata that *Bhagavad Gita* was revealed by Lord Krishna to Arjuna. The day was an *Ekadshi* day of *Margshirsha* month in the Hindu Calendar.

'Arjuna, whenever righteousness is on the decline, unrighteousness is in the ascendant, then I body Myself forth. 'For the protection of the virtuous, for the extirpation of evil-doers, and for establishing Dharma (righteousness) on a firm footing, I manifest Myself from age to age.'

— **Lord Krishna**

Bhagavad Gita, Chapter 4 Verses 7 & 8

Battle of Mahabharata

Now we will understand the battle of Mahabharata that was fought between cousin brothers. This battle lasted for 18 days and few million people died in it. This battle was fought in the field of Kurukshetra (near New Delhi). This was no way an ordinary battle that could have concluded easily. We can understand this if we know the principle warriors on both the sides.

The cousins were the Pandava brothers and the Kauravas brothers. Lord Krishna supported the Pandavas. The fathers of Pandavas and Kauravas were real brothers. Then there was a grandfather Bhishma who fought from the side of the Kauravas.

Let us familiarise ourselves with some of these warriors to understand that this was no way an ordinary war.

Bhishma Pitamah (the grand old man of the Kauravas race) was son of Ganga (River Ganges). He is one of the most significant persons of the *Mahabharata* and it is important to know about him. His father wanted to go for a second marriage after Ganga disappeared from the earth but the father of the girl did not agree as he felt Bhishma will be next King. So Bhishma took a vow that he will not marry in his life and keeping his promise, he did not marry. He was blessed by his father that he will die only when he wished to die which meant no one could kill him, so irrespective of the strength of the army, he could not be killed. He brought up the children of Pandavas and Kauravas with lot of love and affection never realizing that they will end up in a battleground one day. Above all, he also had to helplessly participate in that war.

Pandavas were 5 brothers, all blessed, honest and truthful; they were incarnations of Heavenly Gods. Kauravas were jealous of the Pandavas and constantly plotted against them. Ultimately, they went to war for the sovereignty of the kingdom.

Bhishma had taken another vow that he would always support the King sitting on the throne of Hastinapur. While the elder brother of the Pandavas deserved to be the King, Kauravas manipulated and took the kingdom. They also insulted their cousins, banished them to the forests for 14 years and insulted their wife in the court.

Bhishma was caught in his vows, not knowing that these vows will become so much a pain for him. He blessed the Pandavas for victory and desired that he himself is defeated and killed in the battle so he could be relieved from the pain.

In the battlefield, Bhishma was made incapable to fight with arrows piercing through all over his body. So, he was physically not in a position to fight. He was one of the rare souls who knew that Krishna was a complete Lord so he knew that the Lord would find a way to Bhishma's death, as he did not want to support the King who was on a wrong path. Unfortunately, he was bound by his vow.

When Lord Krishna declared that He will not lift any weapon during the war, Bhishma challenged Lord Krishna that he will make Him lift the weapon. Lord Krishna smiled. Only a true devotee can challenge God. History and all scriptures have proved that when devotees challenge God, devotees always win. God is strong but not emotionally strong enough to win His true devotees. Love has to show its strength too, which is also His creation. Bhishma Pitamah had taken another vow that he will not kill any of the Pandava brothers. They were his grandchildren and on the right spiritual path.

Arjuna fought with Bhishma Pitamah but could no way have defeated Bhishma Pitamah. Arjuna also hurled arrows on Bhishma Pitamaha in a very disinterested manner so that they did not hurt him. Lord Krishna saw this, and dismounted the chariot, picked up the wheel of a broken chariot and was about to kill Bhishma Pitamah when Arjuna fell on Lord

Krishna's feet and reminded him that Lord had vowed not to pick any weapon during the war. But at the same time, Bhishma saw an opportunity to get killed by Lord Krishna so he went right in front of Krishna to make it easy for the Lord to kill him. But finally Lord did not kill Him as Arjuna stopped Lord Krishna.

On his death bed, Bhishma Pitamah complained to Lord Krishna as to why Lord did not kill him. Lying on his death bed of arrows Bhishma Pitamah asked Lord Krishna on where he went wrong in his life. Lord said, 'Is this answer good enough if I say that I know you were not wrong.' Satisfied with the answer from Lord Krishna, he peacefully passed away.

After the death of his mother, Bhishma visited her (River Ganges) very often whenever he saw some unfairness being done by the King and Kauravas against the Pandavas. Once Mother Ganges told Bhishma that he did not ask for permission from her before he took the vow. At this Bhishma told his mother that he would not come to her after that moment, in fact mother would come to him the next time. When he was on his death bed, Bhishma asked Arjuna to get him some water as he was thirsty. Arjuna brought water from River Ganges by piercing the earth with his arrow. Ganges was hundreds of miles away but with one arrow he could bring that water through the earth for Bhishma. Such was the power and blessing which these warriors mustered on the battlefield of Kurukshetra.

The complete conspiracy on how to plan and kill Bhishma Pitamah was planned by Bhisham Pitamah himself and revealed to Pandavas when they approached Bhishma Pitamah to know how they should plan to kill him because there was no way they could win the battle with Bhisham Pitamah in the battlefield. Bhishma Pitamah told them that if there is a woman on Arjuna's chariot, then he will not fight. But Krishna advised Shikhandi to be with Arjuna on his chariot who was neither a man nor a woman. That day, Bhishma did not use his arrows and was defeated by Arjuna, who was remorseful as he wounded Bhishma Pitamah.

While Arjuna understood that Krishna is complete incarnation of God or God Himself on the day when *Bhagavad Gita* was revealed, Bhishma as a devotee knew Lord much earlier.

Karan was another supreme personality who fought from the side of Kauravas. He was the son of the Sun God, so was very brave and undefeatable. He was the elder brother of Pandavas but no one knew this secret except Lord Krishna. Karan himself came to know about it just before the battle. The only other person who knew this was mother Kunti, who was the mother of the Pandavas.

Karan was a big challenge for Arjuna and Arjuna could not have killed Karan. Since Karan knew that Arjuna was his younger brother, he did not kill Arjuna when there was a moment when he could have killed Arjuna. Kauravas elder brother Duryodhana saw that they were losing this battle and he also saw that Karan did not kill Arjuna.

Then there was Dronacharya who was Guru and Mentor of the Pandavas and the Kauravas and taught them the skills for the war as was taught to all the princes at that time. He could not be defeated by anyone. While honest and truthful, he was bound with the kingdom and had to support Kauravas much against his will. He blessed the Pandavas for victory and the blessings of such devout people had to work. He also desired that the Pandavas win as that was the right thing to happen.

There was also a spiritual master named Kripacharya who fought from the Kauravas side but blessed the Pandavas for victory. He was the priest of the family and could have no way been outdone by anyone. He was another honest, blessed and truthful soul fighting from the side of the Kauravas and wishing the victory of the Pandavas.

So all these principle, matchless and valiant warriors stood with the Kauravas but they all desired their own death and defeat and victory of the righteous, i.e. they all blessed the Pandavas for victory.

Mother of the Kauravas was Gandhari who never wished that her children should do anything wrong in life. She was a very pious lady and a devotee of Lord Shiva. Her sacrifice was unparalleled. She was married to King Dhritrashtra who was blind by birth. On the day of their marriage, she covered her eyes so that she should not see as her husband could not see. All her life, she prayed that her children should not do anything wrong but the children did not obey. Her own brother always misguided her children.

While very pious, truthful and honest, she was after all the mother of the Kauravas. So she had blessed her elder son before the war. It was not easy even for Lord Krishna to challenge her but there was no other way for the Lord but to eradicate the wrong doings from the earth and her children were bringing wickedness on the earth.

Gandhari was pure and devotee of Lord Shiva and had known the power of Krishna. At the end of the war when all the Kauravas were killed and many people in the war had been killed, she cursed Krishna. She cursed Krishna as she said that it was only Krishna who could have helped to avoid this war and such a disaster would not have happened. She cursed Krishna that all His caste people will also fight among themselves like the Pandavas and the Kauravas fought and they will kill each other. She also cursed that Lord Krishna would also be killed in an unreligious manner.

Lord Krishna blessed Gandhari and accepted the curses and He planned His own end and the end of the families as per mother Gandhari's curse. This was a hard part of Lord Krishna's incarnation. The Lord has to go through hardships to eradicate sin from the earth.

Now as we progress with the book, we will also see the role of Destiny that is written by individuals themselves according to their Nature and Karmas and is planned, monitored and executed by God's system.

Mahabharata was also a destiny that took shape in *Dwaparayuga* and individuals had to play their roles according to their Nature, their Karma and their destiny.

Now let's come back to the Pandavas. Lord Krishna who said that he would not fight but would just drive the chariot of Arjuna was present with the Pandavas. No one knew who Lord Krishna was, not even Arjuna while they all lived together for many years till Lord Krishna revealed His identity to Arjuna during the battlefield. The teachings of Lord Krishna to Arjuna during the battlefield are in the form of *Bhagavad Gita* and thus our book is also based on teachings and messages from *Bhagavad Gita*.

Arjuna was the principle warrior from the Pandavas side Arjuna was so highly blessed that he collected the key weapons for this battle from Goddess Durga. Arjuna was *Gudakesh* and he did not sleep all through the 18 days of the war. He was *savyasachin* and could hurl the arrows from his left hand as skilfully as he would do with right hand.

So this battle was no way a measure of who had a huge army or who had advanced weapons, rather it was a war of spiritually blessed humans who could not be slain with technological strength.

That is where Lord Krishna had to appear in this battle so that it reached a conclusion and it was proved that the right will eventually win. Main warriors from the Kauravas side also blessed Pandavas for victory as that is where truth prevailed.

Mother Radha
Consort and Soul of Krishna

*Hare Krishna Hare Krishna, Krishna Krishna Hare Hare
Hare Rama Hare Rama, Rama Rama Hare Hare.*

One name of Radha is Hara. She is the internal power of Lord Krishna. Radha is worshipped with Lord Krishna in this *Mahamantra* chanted by Krishna Devotees. Mahamantra means complete devotion. This chanting is treated as complete chanting of God. Radha is worshipped like Krishna.

Radha and Krishna are worshipped together all over the world. Without the mother Radha, Krishna is incomplete. Radha was born 11 months before Lord Krishna. She lived in a village called Barsana. Radha's father was king of the village Barsana. Barsana and Gokul are close to each other.

According to one belief, Radha was found floating on a leaf in a pond in the same village by her father. Radha did not open her eyes for many months. She opened her eyes the first time when Lord Krishna was in front of her.

Like Krishna's birth is celebrated as Krishna Janamashtami, Radha's birth is celebrated as Radha Ashtmi. Radha is a consort of Lord Krishna.

Radha – Krishna

Vrindavan where Radha and Krishna lived stays alive day and night with chanting of Radha's name. When the people in Vrindavan need to draw someone's attention they say 'Radhe-Radhe'. One can feel the blessings of Radha all over in Vrindavan.

Radha Ashtmi is celebrated with as much pomp and show as Krishna Janamashtami. Radha Ashtmi comes 15 days after Krishna Ashtmi. In fact devotees say that Krishna Ashtmi is only an indication that Radha Ashtmi is coming soon. Krishna can be reached with devotion to Radha and Krishna together.

Krishna devotees follow many scriptures from Hinduism.

Bhagavad Gita was revealed by Lord Krishna Himself and this book is based on teachings from *Srimad Bhagavad Gita*.

Srimad Bhagvatam, written by Rishi Veda Vyas is another very blissful scripture chanted and followed by Krishna devotees. This scripture is worshipped like *Bhagavad Gita*. Rishi Veda Vyas worshipped mother Radha for 12 years and then Radha blessed Rishi Veda Vyas to write a scripture and that is *Srimad Bhagvatam*. The source of bliss in *Srimad Bhagvatam* comes from mother Radha.

These two scriptures are possibly the most revered scriptures by Krishna Devotees and one must read them for blessings from Radha and Krishna. One is revealed by Lord Himself and the other is written with blessings by mother Radha.

Harivansha Purana is one of the 18 Puranas of Sanatan Dharma and is worshipped in Hinduism for getting the blessings of Lord Krishna for a noble, high-soul son in the family. Harivansha Purana covers all the dynasties of Lord Hari. Hence the couple that reads this Purana is bound to be blessed.

Radharani has many names according to Her qualities:

Krishnamayi
Govinda-Mohini
Govinda-Sarvasa
Govinda-Snandini
Shiromani Sarva-kanta

Radharani is also known as Sarva-kanti, which indicates that all the beauty and lustre rest in Her body, and all the Lakshmis derive their beauty from Her. Sarva-kanti also means that all the desires of Lord Krishna rest in Srimati Radharani. As Lord Krishna enchants the world with His beauty and charm, Sri Radha enchants Him. Therefore She is the Supreme Goddess. Sri Radha is the full power, and Lord Krishna is the possessor of full power. Thus, the two are no different, as the sunshine is no different from the sun, or as the energy is no different from the energetic or source of energy.

Radhe tu bad bhagini, Kyon tapsya keen tenn lok taran tarad, tere hee Adheen

Without Radharani there is no meaning to Lord Krishna and without Krishna there is no meaning to Radharani. For this reason, in the Vaishnava tradition we always pay respect first to the Lord's internal energy in the form of Radharani, and then to Lord Krishna. Thus, they are referred to as Radha-Krishna, or as Sita-Rama, Lakshmi-Narayana, and so on. In this way, Radha and Krishna are one, but when Lord Krishna wants to enjoy, He manifests Himself as Radharani. Otherwise, there is no energy in which Krishna can attain pleasure outside Himself.

Among the gopis of Vrindavana, Srimati Radharani *and another* gopi are considered the chief ones. However, when we compare the gopis, it appears that Srimati Radha Rani is most important because Her real feature expresses the highest ecstasy of love. The ecstasy of love experienced by the other gopis cannot be compared to that of Srimati Radharani.

Vrindawan ke vrikh ko, Maram na jane koie Jaha dal dal or pat pat pe, Shri Radhe Radhe hoia

Radha's love towards Krishna in the terrestrial or customary meaning is not just the relation between a man and woman, rather the feeling of this love is divine and phenomenal which gives it a pious form. The philosophical side of this reduces the distance of the support and supportive, also the difference between the worshipper and worshipful is not there. Krishna is the life of Vraj; Radha is the soul of Krishna. That is why, it is said, *'Atma Tu Radhika Tasya'* (Radha, you are His soul). One form of Radha is, she is a devotee, worshipper of Krishna and in the second form she is the worshipful, devoted by Krishna. *'Aradhyate Asau itii Radha.'* Radha – Krishna's love is the symbol of the feeling of being united.

In the Brihad-Gautamiya Tantra, Radha is described as follows: "The transcendental goddess Srimati Radha Rani is the direct counterpart of Lord Sri Krishna. She is the central figure for all the goddesses of fortune. She possesses all the attractiveness to attract the all-attractive Personality of Godhead. She is the primeval internal potency of the Lord."

Radha has many meaningful names that describe her qualities and characteristics.

- **Radhika** - This is the most common name, meaning she whose worship of the Krishna is all powerful. She who embodies supreme focus and mental clarity. The incarnation of the goddess Lakshmi. Beauty, intelligence, and a fortunate one.
- **Gandharvi** - Expert singer.
- **Govinda-nandini** - She who gives happiness to Govinda (Krishna).
- **Govinda-mohini** - She who mystifies Govinda
- **Govinda-sarvasva** - One to whom Govinda is the all-in-all, or everything.

- **Sarva-kanta Shiromani** - The crown jewel among all of Krishna's consorts.
- **Krishnamayi** - The one who sees Krishna both within and without.
- **Madan-Mohan-Mohini** - Within Gaudiya tradition Krishna (as the Supreme Person) is believed to be the enchanter of all living beings, including even Kamadeva (Madan)—The god of attraction. Because Radha has the unique position of being able to enchant even Krishna she is therefore known as Madan-Mohan-Mohini: *the enchanter of the enchanter of Cupid.*
- **Aradhana** - The root name of Radha Rani, meaning one who excels in worshiping Krishna.
- **Sarva-lakshmi** - The original source of all the goddesses of fortune.
- **Vrshabhanu-nandini** - Daughter of Vrishabanu.
- **Vrshabhanu-suta** - Daughter of Vrishabanu.
- **Vrshabhanu-Dulari** - loving daughter of Vrishabanu.
- **Vrndavaneshvari** - Queen of Vrindavana.
- **Lalita-Sakhi** - Friend of the gopi Lalita.
- **Gokula-Taruni** - She whom all young girls of Gokul worship
- **Damodara Rati** - She who dresses herself to please Damodara (Krishna)
- **Radharani** – Radha the queen
- **Radha-Krishna** - Krishna Himself in the form of Radha (Worship of Krishna with Radha)
- **Vrajrani** - Queen of Vraj (Krishna being the king)
- **Swaminiji**- The companion of Krishna

- **Karika** - Mix form of Krishna and Radha; Verse; Reborn
- **Ramika**_Reborn; New Face; Modern
- **Sakalepsitdaatri**- She fulfils all desires of her devotees.
- **Raaseshwari** - The goddess of *raas* (folk-dance).
- **Sarveshwari** - The one who is goddess of all.
- **Raj-Rajeshwari** - The goddess of god.
- **Ladali** - The beloved.
- **Barsaane Wali** - The one who lives at Barsaana.
- **Krishna-Priya** - Beloved of Lord Krishna.
- **Haridaas-Dulari** - Beloved of swami Haridas

Temple Deities in India and abroad are generally named in order of Radharani first and then Krishna. Krishna is approachable through the mercy of Srimati Radharani and no one else. So for example, if one were to enter the Govindaji temple in Vrindavan the Deities are named Radha Govinda and devotees of Krishna would pray to Radha and Govinda not just Krishna. This is because Krishna is controlled by Radharani's love.

Radha used to worship Lord Krishna and derive immense joy and pleasure in chanting His name. Lord Krishna noticed the devotion that Radha had and how she was blessed by chanting Krishna's name. Lord Krishna Himself did not ever derive that level of enjoyment as Radha did.

To get a taste of the same pleasure, it is believed that Lord Krishna appeared back on earth as Chaitanya Mahaprabhu in the moods of Radharani and chanted Lord Krishna's name. Lord Chaitanya Mahaprabhu is often named as Gaura and Nimai.

Chaitanya has left one written record in Sanskrit called *Siksastakam*. Chaitanya's epistemological, theological and ontological teachings are summarised as ten roots or maxims (*dasa mula*). The statements of amnaya (scripture) are the chief proof. By these statements the following ten topics are taught.

1. Krishna is the Supreme Absolute Truth.
2. Krishna is endowed with all energies.
3. Krishna is the ocean of rasa (theology).
4. The *jivas* (individual souls) are all separated parts of the Lord.
5. In bound state the jivas are under the influence of matter, due to their *tatastha* nature.
6. In the liberated state the jivas are free from the influence of matter, due to their tatastha nature.
7. The jivas and the material world are both different from and identical to the Lord.
8. Pure devotion is the practice of the jivas.
9. Pure love of Krishna is the ultimate goal.
10. Hare krishna hare krishna krishna krishna hare hare hare ram hare ram ram ram hare hare
11. Krishna is the only lovable blessing to be received.

'Though birthless and immortal and the Lord of all beings, I manifest Myself through My own Yogamaya (divine potency), keeping My nature (Prakriti) under control.'

— Lord Krishna

Bhagavad Gita, Chapter 4 Verse 6

Yogamaya
Sister of Lord Krishna

When lord Krishna was born to Devaki and Vasudeva, Yogamaya was born to Nand and mother Yashoda. Children were exchanged by Nand and Vasudeva and Lord Krishna became the son of Nand and Yashoda. Yogamaya is Goddess Durga.

Srimad-Bhagvatam Canto 10.1 to 10.13 explains, 'Durga is not different from Yogamaya. When one understands Durga properly, he is immediately liberated, for Durga is originally the spiritual potency, by whose mercy one can understand the Supreme Personality of Godhead very easily.'

There is a difference between Yogamaya and Mahamaya. Yogamaya manages the spiritual world, and by her partial expansion as Mahamaya she manages the material world.

As stated in the Narada-pancaratra, Mahamaya is partial expansion of Yogamaya. The Narada-pancaratra clearly states that the Supreme Personality has one potency, which is sometimes described as Durga.

The Brahma-samhita says, chayeva yasya bhuvanani bibharti durga 'Durga is not different from Yogamaya".

When one understands Durga properly, he is immediately liberated, for Durga is originally the spiritual potency, by whose mercy one can understand the Supreme Personality of Godhead very easily.

The Mahamaya-sakti, however, is a covering of Yogamaya, and she is therefore called the covering potency. By this covering potency, the entire material world is bewildered. In conclusion, bewildering the conditioned souls and liberating the devotees are both functions belonging to Yogamaya.

Yogamaya is Lord Krishna's divine potency.

'*Veiled by My Yogamaya, My divine potency, I am not manifest to all. Hence these ignorant folk fail to recognize Me, the birthless and imperishable Supreme Deity, i.e. consider Me as subject to birth and death*'

— **Lord Krishna**

Bhagavad Gita, Chapter 7 Verse 25

Gopis worshipped Durga and their prayers were to get Krishna as their husband. Durga that Gopis worshipped is Yogamaya, the internal potency of Lord Krishna as Gopis were not attracted to any material substance.

We can understand that the internal and external, or superior and inferior, potencies of the Supreme Lord are personified as Yoga-maya and Mahamaya, respectively. The name Durga is sometimes used to refer to the internal, superior potency, as stated in the Pañcaratra: 'In all mantras used to worship Krishna, the presiding deity is known as Durga.' Thus in the transcendental sound vibrations glorifying and worshiping the Absolute Truth, Krishna, the presiding deity of the particular mantra or hymn is called Durga. The name Durga therefore refers also to that personality who functions as the internal potency of the Lord and who is thus on the platform of *suddha-sattva*, pure transcendental existence. This internal potency is understood to be Krishna's sister, known also as Ekanamsa or Subhadra. This is the Durga who was worshiped by the gopis in Vrindavan.

Durga worship is performed with Durga's scripture *Durga Saptashati* which was written before Lord Krishna was born.

Durga Saptashti mentions that in future the birth of Durga will happen as daughter of Nand and Yashoda. This is mentioned as one of the three supreme secrets in Durga Saptashti. This was revealed by Medha Muni to King Surath and Vaishya.

Later, mother Durga and Lord Krishna appeared on one single day on Krishna Janamashtmi. Durga worship is performed on Navratras where devotees fast for 8 to 9 days (Ashtmi or Navami). Navratras come twice a year and are most celebrated in North and West India.

Navratras actually come four times a year. The other two times, Navratras are called Gupt Navratras and fasts are observed by people in deep devotion of Maa Durga.

Durga Saptshloki is a short but complete worship of Durga. This was revealed by Lord Shiva to Mata Parvati. Mother Durga should be worshipped with Durga Saptashati and by observing Navratras fasts twice every year.

In Durga Saptshati, there is a beautiful worship of mother Durga. When Durga removed all the sufferings of the Devtas, she asked Devtas on what other blessing they need. Devtas were in full devotion and did not need anything else but they asked mother Durga on how they can get the highest blessing from mother. Mother Durga herself revealed that if she is worshipped by these 32 names, she will relieve the worshipper from all the pains and she said that this was a worship that highly pleases mother Durga.

1	**Durgā**	The Reliever of Difficulties
2.	**Durgātirśaminī**	Who puts difficulties at peace
3.	**Durgāpadvinivārinī**	Dispeller of difficult adversities
4.	**Durgamacchedinī,**	Who cuts down difficulty
5.	**Durgasādhinī**	The performer of Discipline to expel difficulties
6.	**Durganāśinī**	The Destroyer of Difficulty
7.	**Durgatoddhārinī**	Who holds the whip of difficulties
8.	**Durgenihantrī,**	Who sends difficulties to Ruin
9.	**Durgamāpahā**	Who measures difficulties
10.	**Durgamajñānadā**	Who makes difficulties unconscious
11.	**Durgadaityalokadavānalā**	Who destroys the world of difficult thoughts
12.	**Durgamā**	The mother of difficulties

13.	**Durgamālokā**	The perception of difficulties
14.	**Durgamātmasvarūpinī**	The Intrinsic Nature of the soul of difficulties
15.	**Durgamārgapradā**	Who searches through the difficulties
16.	**Durgamavidyā**	The knowledge of difficulties
17.	**Durgamāśritā**	The Extrication from difficulties
18.	**Durgamajñānasamsthānā**	The continued existence of difficulties
19.	**Durgamadhyānabhāsinī**	Whose meditation remains brilliant when in difficulties
20.	**Durgamohā**	Who deludes difficulties
21.	**Durgamagā**	Who resolves difficulties
22.	**Durgamārthasvarūpiṇī**	Who is the intrinsic nature of the object of difficulties
23.	**Durgamāsurasanhantrī**	The annihilator of the egotism of difficulties
24.	**Durgamāyudhadhāriṇī**	Bearer of the weapon against difficulties
25.	**Durgamāṅgī**	The refinery of difficulties

26.	**Durgamatā**	Who is beyond difficulties
27.	**Durgamyā**	This present difficulty
28.	**Durgameśvarī**	The empress of difficulties
29.	**Durgabhīmā**	Who is terrible to difficulties
30.	**Durgabhāmā**	The lady to difficulties
31.	**Durgabhā**	The illuminator of difficulties
32.	**Durgadāriṇī**	Who cuts off difficulties

'Arjuna, all the worlds from Brahmaloka (the heavenly realm of the Creator, Brahma) downwards are liable to birth and rebirth, But, O son of Kunti, on attaining Me there is no rebirth (For, while I am beyond Time, regions like Brahmaloka, being conditioned by time, are transitory).

— **Lord Krishna**

Bhagavad Gita, Chapter 8 Verse 16

Blessings by Birth

We start with blessings by birth. Some become very rich by birth because they are born in rich families and some are starving. Some are born in families of enlightened people who advise them humbleness; spirituality, sacrifice by birth and some get an environment by birth that has all sorts of conflicts.

We do not pay much attention to births in lower worlds like animals, insects as we feel these are different species and have got nothing to do with humans. No, they were humans and they will be human beings again. That means we can also get there.

Then there are births that we can't see but we hear these from our elders that there is heaven and that there are other worlds as well. Yes, scriptures talk about all these worlds.

Now comes a fourth world and probably that was one of the reasons that *Bhagavad Gita* was revealed to Arjuna in the field of Kurukshetra. Mention of this fourth world is not obvious in many scriptures but Lord Krishna revealed this clearly in *Bhagavad Gita*. This world is above Time. This world is Home of God. This world does not change with time. If you see Time is the ruler for this world. Everything is changing with Time. We are heading towards completing journey in this body and the Time available is less than a hundred years for a new born today. For Sun, it is millions of years but when we say millions of years, we still talk time. Ever wonder a talk that has no mention of Time. That is this fourth world—painless, beautiful, self-illumined, all peaceful, nothing changes—that is God's home and in *Bhagavad Gita* Lord Krishna told Arjuna that you can get there. Now that is a beautiful destination to aim for. Will we get there; answer is yes for one in a million who is sincere in his determination to get there.

Now this is where the question of journey comes up. We have seen four types of worlds. Journey with this body will take us to one of these four destinations. This calls for a detailed knowledge on what should be done to get to the Fourth world. Now a question comes up and the same question came to Arjuna's mind 'what happens if I fail?' If you have started the journey in the right direction and death meets you before you reach that destination or God's home, then there is no worry as you have completed some journey with this body and the rest you will be able to cover with the new body. Worry is if you have started your journey in a wrong direction or in an opposite direction, then in the next birth you will be much further away from Lord's home than you were in this birth. Like, if you start your journey towards south and your destination is 100 miles away, if you cover 30 miles and then night falls and you sleep, so when you get up you are only 70 miles away because you have covered 30 miles on the previous day. Same is the status of journey for human births.

So journey in the right direction is very important. Once rules of the journey are set in the right direction, then it is a matter of commitment on how fast one can run to reach that destination in one birth.

The most beautiful aspect of *Bhagavad Gita* is that advancement of journey in right direction is very painless. It does not call for leaving your home or painful penances. It is the same work, same job, same natural duties performed differently. Once you practice that, you will observe how easy it was and how real it was and how accurate it was. It got to be because that is defined by the Lord and when the Lord speaks, He understands your position as He is the one who has created you; He is the one who has defined rules of the game called life.

Now this means that whatever we got by birth has come with blessings determined by where we left our last journey. It is just an indication of where we were when we existed in our last birth. What discontinued was memory, what discontinued was material richness. If one is very rich in this birth and he did not cover the journey in the right direction, he could get to miseries in next birth because material journey discontinues after death. And if for some reason, he is born in lower worlds of insects and animals, this material richness is anyway meaningless.

What are the key blessings or curse we have when we are born, i.e. what we brought from our previous births. Now previous birth may not be just the last birth but will be last many births and their cumulative has shown up in this birth.

These are the things that we carry from birth to birth.

First is our Nature, which is broadly combination of Anger, Ego and Desire. If you were an angry person in your last birth, you will be born as an angry person in this birth. If you had very high desire for material attraction, you will be born with the same feelings in this birth. Look at some of the most successful people around and you may find that they are very angry people. They are successful because they are intelligent and tell them to control their anger, they will fail as even with all the success, they have no control on their anger. In God's system, Anger is bad and will eventually take you to the lower worlds so you see how different the rules are. In this material richness journey, they feel one of the reasons of their success is anger and in the spiritual journey, they are advancing towards lower worlds every day. Anger, Ego and Desire are friends. They promote each other. If desire is increased then Ego and Anger will also grow.

Why is anger bad? You often hurt people. When you hurt people, they carry the same unpleasantness home and to their society and to their teams. You create an unpleasant environment in God's beautiful home. You take people away from Him. You become a source of bad inspiration and when you do it every day, you cover some journey away from his home every day. You are being identified as the key source for creation of a bad and unholy environment.

Second is Actions that are well-defined in *Bhagavad Gita* as Karmas. Karmas mean Action. Every action that we perform is a Karma. When we hurt people, it is Karma. When we love people, it is Karma. When we eat, when we feed poor, when we respect elders, when we cheat, when we lie, when we sacrifice, when we speak humble….every act is a Karma. Karmas decide destiny. So, our birth and blessings by birth were decided by our previous Karmas. When we say God decided, what do we mean by God's decision? He is not going to do favours. He has a system and that system works. His system decides the blessings by birth based on our previous Karmas.

Now let us relate Karmas (Actions) to Nature. If your Nature is hurting and full of anger, you cannot perform Good Karmas. If you think you can, that itself shows that you defined your own rules and His rules are different. When it comes to continuity of journey to next birth, all our defined rules will suddenly become meaningless. His system will take over and get us to our next birth based on our Karmas and Nature. Nature influences Karmas and you will also find that you got no control on your nature and we will come to the teachings of *Bhagavad Gita* on how do we control nature and perform good karmas as per His rules and not as per rules of this material world.

Third is our attraction towards God as we see that some people are naturally attracted towards God. You will find they are mostly humble if they are genuine lovers of God. This is key point in the journey that we were talking about when we said that a person has moved 30 miles towards south. So the attraction and meditation puts you in the right direction. When you start moving towards the right direction, right Nature and right Karmas naturally come along and together and they make a powerful and forceful combination to help you move in the right direction.

Material richness and spiritual richness (attraction towards God) is very different. One materially rich person may also be a spiritually rich person and another materially rich person may have no knowledge of spiritual path. Both may be very successful in their field. One may be advancing his journey towards God's home every day and another may be moving away from His home every day, while both of them may be getting materially richer every day. See the difference in rules.

Bhagavad Gita talks about King Janaka as the most advanced Karma Yogi. He was a King and has a special mention in *Bhagavad Gita* and he is the only Karma Yogi mentioned in *Bhagavad Gita* who knew how to stay detached to material richness. Despite having all the material richness, he continued on advancing in his journey towards God.

Now Fourth is Destiny. Destiny is nothing but cumulative latencies of previous births—good and bad. Destiny could mean that a person is blind, met with an accident at an early age, suffers from something, and has unsuccessful relationships despite no fault in this birth. These are called some pre-determined happenings to the individual based on what he carried forward from the previous birth. In *Bhagavad Gita*, when we explain in detail, these are called Daiva.

'The following are the factors operating towards the accomplishment of actions, viz., the body and the doer, the organs of different functions of manifold kinds; and the fifth is Daiva, latencies of past actions.'

— Lord Krishna

Bhagavad Gita, Chapter 18 Verse 14

When destiny which is a result of cumulative latencies of previous births hits, the person gets helplessly driven into it and performs that activity perforce. Even if he does not want to perform that activity, he ends up performing that activity as if no choice because it was pre-written according to his own Karmas. So Karmas are supreme. They write destiny.

Soul Migration to New Body

Now all this is carried on Soul that migrates from one birth to another birth. Soul is always pure because that is God. Soul is just a carrier of all the above to the next birth. Soul is pure God. It cannot get impure. Soul's age is more than that of Sun, Moon and Earth. This is the Soul that enlightened people's reach within their bodies. This is the soul where they see God, they talk to God. Soul records everything that we do and is witness to all our Karmas and hence decides the destiny.

'As a man shredding worn-out garments, takes other new ones, likewise, the embodied soul, casting off worn-out bodies, enters into others that are new.'

— Lord Krishna

Bhagavad Gita, Chapter 2 Verse 22

Now since the migration happens to Higher Worlds, Humans births, Animal worlds and God's home with the same Soul so it means that Animals also have a soul like Human Beings. They also get hurt. They are there because of their Karmas, and Destiny took them there. Destiny can do the same to anyone.

Scriptures are a wake-up call to move in the right direction. Even if one is going in a wrong direction and he realises this at some point in life, he should feel that he is a blessed soul and it means that God loves him and is giving him an opportunity to change direction and move in the right direction. This may be a result of some good past Karmas. You walk every day in some direction because you perform Karmas every day. So, you write your Destiny every day. Some people feel that old age is the best age to catch up on these things, while no age is late rather the journey in the right direction should start as soon as one gets the awareness on this.

Reading the Holy Scripture of *Bhagavad Gita* is a blessing that comes only to the deserving few.

'Hardly any great soul perceives this soul as marvellous, scarce another great soul likewise speaks thereof as marvellous, and scarce another worthy one hears of it as marvellous, while there are some who know it not even on hearing of it'.

— **Lord Krishna**

Bhagavad Gita, Chapter 2 Verse 29

Lord Krishna has clearly stated above that only a Worthy one hears of it as marvellous. As you read the scripture, you find who that worthy one is. Who is the one who has a basic nature and entitlement to go to God's home and if one does not have, then how can one change to become entitled.

Blessings by Birth

Our journey now starts in this birth with a lot of cumulative remains of the past births based on our Karmas (Actions) in previous births, Nature of Anger-Ego-Desire, State of Meditation, pre-defined destinies etc. and we have to excel in this birth with all these blessings, curses, gifts and shortcomings. If you take His support and stay focused on Him, you will go through all this with no difficulty.

Four Destinations
After This Journey

Param Dham – God's Abode – Above Time

Higher Worlds – Heaven etc.

Human Birth

Lower Worlds – Animal Births

There are four types of births mentioned in *Bhagavad Gita*. It actually talks of three births because going to God's Home after death does not result in a new birth so there are four destinations and three types of births.

First one is God's Home above Time. Some rare soul goes and merges with Him and goes above Time. These will be few enlightened souls in the whole world.

Second is going to Higher Worlds. This means Heaven, Sun Lok and other higher worlds gifted with lot of pleasures and enjoyments. After the merits are exhausted, souls return back to earth, even Brahmaloka, which is considered to be the highest of all. It is subject to birth and death after a certain time which is practically millions of equivalent years on earth.

Third world is the world of Human Beings. This world is great as all gates are open only from this birth, i.e. whether you go to God's Home, or go to Higher Worlds, or born back as Human beings or go to the lower worlds of animals and species.

Within Human births, you see as many types of births as number of people. Some are highly blessed, some are rich, some are suffering every day, some have unbearable pains, some are wasting this blessedness by spending time in all worldly enjoyments and some are devoted to sacrifice all the time and yet not satisfied and want to do more. Some are sitting in Himalayas in search of God, some are billionaires working hard every day to add few more millions to their fortune and so on.

Fourth world is considered to be the lower worlds. A world of Animals and Insects. This birth is only for suffering for a defined period. Now the defined period is very alarming and it could be million years. That means some of the mistakes and blunders performed as Humans could take one to lower worlds for million years. Similarly, a little caution, commitment, sacrifice, sincerity, renunciation could take one to His Home which is all peace and you are delivered from the pains of old Age, re-birth and disease.

Knowing the reality of Time is very relevant. You can afford to do no mistake. During the Time cycle, at coming of the cosmic nightfall, all embodied beings merge into the same subtle body of Brahma, known as the unmanifest.

'Far beyond even this unmanifest, there is yet another unmanifest Existence, that Supreme Divine person who does not perish even though all beings perish. The same unmanifest which has been spoken of as the Indestructible, is also called the supreme goal; that again is My supreme Abode, attaining which they return not to this mortal world'

— **Lord Krishna**

Bhagavad Gita, Chapter 8 Verse 20 & 21

They do not return to this mortal world because they are liberated. They are no more subjected to the cycles of birth and death. They neither go to Heaven to enjoy the fruits of their merits, nor do they go to the lower worlds of animals as a result of wrong doings. They rise above all this. In the subsequent pages, we talk about how God cautioned that people looking for God cannot do the actions that result in taking them to Heaven as there is no way to God's Home from heaven. People ascending to Heaven return back to the world of Humans on earth and once again go through the complete cycle of birth and death.

'Those who are votaries of gods, go to gods, those who are votaries of manes, reach the manes; those who adore the spirits, reach the spirits and those who worship Me, come to Me alone. That is why My devotees are no longer subject to birth and death.'

— **Lord Krishna**

Bhagavad Gita, Chapter 9 Verse 25

Again lord talks about defining your journey. Those who are votaries of gods, go to gods. Those who are votaries of spirits reach spirits. This shows that each human being defines his next destination within this birth. It is so obvious from Lord Krishna's blissful messages that within this birth—consciously or unconsciously you define your next destination. When we say unconsciously, it means that our spiritual knowledge may not be complete and perfect. Hence the need for right knowledge comes again. So knowledge is very important, so one is conscious of what he is doing and where he is headed in his current journey.

Three Gunas Three Destinations
(Own soul is witness)

We defined four destinations after this journey is completed and three types of re-births. One destination which is destination to God's home does not result in re-birth.

So, there are three types of re-births, hence three types of *Gunas* – one for each destination other than God's Home. Now these three Gunas are always playing on each individual trying to prove their individual supremacy as *Bhagavad Gita* defines it.

Three Gunas – Three types of Births. All three are present in each Individual. None is free from them even in the higher worlds. It is only the dominance of the individual Guna more than other two Gunas that decides the destination.

'Only the Purusa in association with Prakrti experiences objects of the nature of the three Gunas evolved from Prakrti and it is attachment with these Gunas that is responsible for the birth of the soul in good and evil wombs'

— Lord Krishna

Bhagavad Gita, Chapter 13 Verse 21

The spirit dwelling in this body, is really the same as the Supreme. He has been spoken of as the Witness, the true Guide, the Sustainer of all, the

Experiencer (as the embodied soul), the Oversoul and the Absolute as well.

— **Lord Krishna**

Bhagavad Gita, Chapter 13 Verse 22

Soul present in each individual is the same. It is a complete God. This soul is witness to everything that we do. It watches us with thousand eyes. It is true guide; yes it is God's presence in us so got to be the true guide. Now here is the difference, the guide is inside us but we decide not to listen to the guide. We listen more to the voice of Gunas and ignore the true guide. Scriptures like *Bhagavad Gita* are meant to invoke the listening capability to this true guide. God means good to us.

Now it is attachment with these Gunas that result in the journey to good and evil wombs. Evil wombs mean that the journey is heading towards a wrong destination. An attachment to *Tamas* ruins the journey and the destination.

'Arjuna, being without beginning and without attributes, this indestructible supreme Spirit, though dwelling in the body, in fact does nothing, nor gets tainted.'

— **Lord Krishna**

Bhagavad Gita, Chapter 13 Verse 31

Soul stays pure. It does not get tainted. It can't because it is God's presence in us. So attachment to Gunas is what defines the next destination. Soul is same for any destination that we may choose – be it Higher Worlds, be it Human beings, be it Lower worlds of Animals and Insects. Now this proves another important point that all these births in lower worlds of animals and insects have the same soul as Humans. God is equally present in them as Human Beings. God is not less present in them. So why they are there is because of their attachment to one of the Gunas that took these souls into these births. So when you hurt an animal, you hurt the same God as you would hurt when you hurt a Human.

Now let us look at the three Gunas

'Sattva, Rajas and Tamas – these three Gunas born of Nature tie down the imperishable soul to the body, Arjuna. Of these Sattva being immaculate, is illuminating and flawless, Arjuna, it binds through attachment to happiness and knowledge. Arjuna, know the quality of Rajas, which is of the nature of passion, as born of desire and attachment. It binds the soul through attachment to actions and their fruit. And know Tamas, the deluder of all those who look upon the body as their own self, as born of ignorance. It binds the soul through error, sleep and sloth, Arjuna.'

— Lord Krishna

Bhagavad Gita, Chapter 14 Verses 5-9

Sattva Guna is pure and flawless and lifts one upwards towards Higher Worlds and towards God's Home.

Rajas Guna binds one with Actions with interested motive. It binds with desires. It binds with all the happiness that can be derived from the material world.

Tamas promotes one towards error. Something not allowed in God's system. Error means error in spiritual system of God.

People living the Sattva life wend their ways upwards. People living a Rajas life stay in the middle, and people living the Tamas life wend their way downwards to the lower worlds.

When Sattva dominates on you, you feel good about everything. You feel blessed by God. You have no complaints. You eat natural food that promotes longevity. Your nature is helping. You see God's presence in everyone. You do not talk ill of anyone. You are naturally attracted towards God. You observe fasts. You derive highest enjoyment through meditation. You do not see belongingness to the material world. You realize the pains in birth, old age, death and disease. You spread love. Your behaviour is humble.

When Rajas dominates on you, you feel restless. You like spicy food. You are attracted towards material things. You need more, you have less. You do not mind bending the spiritual rules to get more. You feel jealous, you do not like the environment and you have many complaints. You need to enjoy a lot in a short time. You want your people to go out of the way to win and make more and more.

When Tamas dominates on you, you love unnatural food which is not meant for Human beings. You want to hurt people. You want to take away the livelihood of the people. You need more even through an ill-legitimate manner. Ill-legitimate means when something is not permissible by a particular set of laws or by the laws of the world as well as by the spiritual system. You are always angry and have a high ego. No one is equal to you and no one dare be equal to you. You like sleeping more, unconscious of the character, you postpone the important deeds. You think this is the smart way of doing things. Ignorance is always dominating on you. One has no belief in God or destination after death. One with tamas gunas comes heavy on God's system.

'Overpowering Rajas and Tamas, Arjuna, Sattva prevails; overpowering Sattva and Tamas, Rajas prevails, even so overpowering Sattva and Rajas, Tamas prevails'

— **Lord Krishna**

Bhagavad Gita, Chapter 14 Verse 10

Sattva, Rajas and Tamas all the time fight within our body for establishing their supremacy. We decide our next destination depending upon with whom do we work and make supreme and whom do we allow to dominate between the three.

If Sattva dominates at the time of death, one goes to the Higher worlds. If Rajas dominates at the time of death, one is re-born as a Human being and if Tamas dominates at the time of death, one goes to the lower worlds of Animals and Insects.

What dominates at the time of death is what has been dominating over the greater period of the life especially towards the later years of one's life. Meditation puts one on the Sattva path. Sattva alone does not take one to God's Home as renunciation is a must for way to God's Home but Sattva keeps the journey on the right track.

'When a man dies during the preponderance of Sattva, he obtains the stainless ethereal worlds (heaven etc.) attained by men of noble deeds'

— Lord Krishna

Bhagavad Gita, Chapter 14 Verse 14

'Dying when Rajas predominates, he is born among those attached to action; even so, the man who has expired during the preponderance of Tamas is reborn in the species of the deluded creatures such as insects and beasts etc.

— Lord Krishna

Bhagavad Gita, Chapter 14 Verse 15

God is above all the three Gunas and all Human Beings, Devtas in Higher Worlds and Animals and Species in lower worlds are influenced and impacted by these three Gunas.

Even Sattvik Guna which is illuminating and flawless is one of these three Gunas which works on an individual to take him to Heaven, gifts all comforts, brings him back in rich and pious families and keeps him revolving in the cycles of birth-death-old age and disease.

At the time of death, Soul takes the domination of the nature of the three Gunas, Karmas and Mind, and as per the status of all these the soul migrates to the new birth in Higher Worlds, human birth or lower worlds.

'Even as the wind wafts scents from their seat, so, too, the Jivatma, which is the controller of the body etc., taking the mind and the senses from the body which it leaves behind, forthwith migrates to the body which it acquires'

— **Lord Krishna**

Bhagavad Gita, Chapter 15 Verse 8

This is God's Maya which consists of all these three Gunas.

'For this most wonderful Maya (veil) of Mine, consisting of the three Gunas (modes of Nature), is extremely difficult to breakthrough; those, however, who constantly adore Me alone, are able to cross it.

— **Lord Krishna**

Bhagavad-Gita, Chapter 7 Verse 14

Heaven is Away from God's Home

'Arjun, those who are full of worldly desires and devoted to the letter of Vedas, who look upon heaven as the supreme goal and argue that there is nothing beyond heaven, are unwise. They utter flowery speech recommending many rituals of various kinds for the attainment of pleasure and power with rebirth as their fruit. Those whose minds are carried away by such words, and who are deeply attached to pleasures and worldly power, cannot attain the determinate intellect concentrated on God'

— **Lord Krishna**

Bhagavad Gita, Chapter 2 Verses 42-44

Vedas, Puranas are our old scriptures and have answer to any of the problems that one may have. Vedas cover the human race journey, heaven and all other worlds. There are various mantras and rituals when performed can result in material gains, power, ascending to Heaven after death and also resulting in re-birth in rich families. Lord cautioned that the people who are following this part of the Vedas are not aiming for God's Home as God's Home is above all these. These rituals and mantras result in lot of material benefit but material benefit is different from spiritual journey.

Bhagavad Gita covers the spiritual journey to God's Home and what one should do to achieve that. Lord says that the people who are following Vedas for material gains should not be mistaken as people working to attain God. They are on a different journey, not on the journey to God's Home.

Now this links to the desires. Lord Krishna mentioned in *Bhagavad Gita* that desires are insatiable like fire. Desires keep growing and you can keep working to meet all the desires but all this collection will be with an individual till his death. If the desires are fulfilled through Mantras and you use the results for goodness of human beings but also grow your desires further, then there is no end, so the journey defined by the individual is to collect maximum ignoring the realization that this is only till the end of the journey of this body.

Time with us in this Human body in this Yuga is defined and we need to be cautious of that.

Dispassion that leads to God's home and how it leads to God's home has been explained well in *Bhagavad Gita*. This had not been covered so well in any scripture. This is one of the key knowledge that one can derive from *Bhagavad Gita*.

'Having enjoyed the extensive heaven-world, they return to this world of mortals on the stock of their merits being exhausted. Thus devoted to the ritual with interested motive, recommended by the three Vedas as the means of attaining heavenly bliss, and seeking worldly enjoyments, they repeatedly come and go (i.e. ascend to heaven by virtue of their merits and return to earth when their fruit has been enjoyed).

— **Lord Krishna**

Bhagavad Gita, Chapter 9 Verse 21

People on the material journey path keep repeating their journey between earth and heaven and are unable to get out of the pain of birth-death, old age and disease and they do not come out of this cycle. So Lord cautioned that people following that part of the Vedas are working for material gains and power only and should not mistake themselves as leading their path to God's home. This is a key message in *Bhagavad Gita* for the ones seeking liberation and where God revealed that this can be best achieved by just doing your natural duties with mediation and dispassion. No need for household people to leave anything and that is the beauty, i.e. getting liberation while performing everything.

'Arjuna, the Vedas thus deal with the evolutes of the three Gunas (modes of Prakrti),viz.,worldly enjoyments and the means of attaining such enjoyment; be thou indifferent to these enjoyments and their means, rising above pairs of opposites like pleasure and pain etc., established in the Eternal Existence (God), absolutely unconcerned about the fulfilment of wants and the preservation of what has been already attained, you be self-controlled'.

— Lord Krishna

Bhagavad-Gita, Chapter 2 Verse 45

Now comes the dispassion which is rising above the opposites like pleasure and pain—not enjoying the pleasure and not suffering the pain. Just establish a connection with Eternal all the time. When you enjoy pleasures, you get attached to pleasures and you need more or at least you need continuity and you get focused on how to get more or maintain what you have got, so attention moves away from God to the pleasures.

A person observing dispassion stays focused on God. He does not worry about the continuity of pleasures because he knows that this journey is not going to go very far, it will at most be with you till you leave the body. His focus is much deeper on where this journey is going to take Him after he leaves this body. When he has that realization, then this pleasure looks meaningless to Him.

He does not go against that like King Janaka who ran the kingdom with dispassion, staying focused on God. He never let the material gains divert attention from God and King Janaka has been quoted in *Bhagavad Gita* as the most spiritual person who performed all his natural duties following detachment with mind fixed on God. When you enjoy pleasures, you also feel the pain. More you enjoy the pleasures, more you feel the pain. This is just natural. So, one keeps swaying between the opposites. However, one who does not enjoy the pleasures, also does not feel the pains. So he is able to stay focused on God during pains as much as he was focused during the pleasures. The more you are swaying between the opposites, lesser you will be attached to God. Lesser the swaying, more will be the focus on God. So, Lord advised to practice self-control.

'A Brahmana, who has obtained enlightenment, has as much use for all the Vedas as one who stands at the brink of a sheet of water overflowing on all sides has for a small reservoir of water'.

— **Lord Krishna**

Bhagavad Gita, Chapter 2 Verse 46

As this journey advances, as the purification starts showing up due to focus on God all the time, having risen above the opposites, inner self gets invoked. When the inner self invokes, light comes from within. Vedas are sitting outside for us to read and for us to go to someone to explain the Vedas to us but the source of Vedas which is Lord is sitting inside us in the form of soul. For a purified intellectual person in the spiritual journey, who has invoked his inner self, the knowledge of Vedas start coming from inside. It just becomes natural for the person that he is able to decide what is right and what is wrong. So, Lord says that the person who has advanced on this journey and has obtained enlightenment has as much use for all the Vedas as one who stands at the brink of a sheet of water overflowing on all sides has for a small reservoir of water. That shows the power of internal awakening which is eternal awakening. This person knows everything naturally. This is again a journey, which is a very easy journey and a very difficult journey as well. It is very easy for the people on the path of meditation and dispassion, while it is a very difficult journey for the people who are unable to control the swing of the opposites.

Desire Clouds Spiritual Knowledge

Eternal enemy of the wise

'As fire is covered by smoke, mirror by dust, and embryo by the amnion, so is knowledge covered by desire'. And, Arjuna, knowledge stands covered by this eternal enemy of the wise, known as desire, which is insatiable like fire. The senses, the mind and the intellect are declared to be its seat; covering the knowledge through these, it (desire) deludes the embodied soul'.

— **Lord Krishna**

Bhagavad Gita, Chapter 3 Verses 38-40

Our desires become hindrance in our spiritual journey. These desires are all worldly desires—short, temporary and can't be met as one desire leads way to another so it never gets over. Lord calls these as 'Eternal enemy of the wise'. These desires lead us to error; these desires ruin the journey and destination. These desires give rise to unwanted Anger and Ego. These desires bring in other enemies to attack our wisdom of spiritual journey. Lord calls it insatiable like fire.

These desires lead to actions with selfish motive. They make you forget what is right in the spiritual journey.

'Arjuna, you must know that what they call Sannyasa is no other than Yoga; for none becomes a Yogi, who has not abandoned his 'Sankalpas' (thoughts of the world).

— **Lord Krishna**

Bhagavad Gita, Chapter 6 Verse 2

'To the contemplative soul who desires to attain Karma Yoga, selfless action is said to be the means; for the same man when he is established in Yoga, absence of all 'Sankalpas' (thoughts of the world) is said to be the way to blessedness.

— **Lord Krishna**

Bhagavad Gita, Chapter 7 Verse 3

'Arjuna, howsoever men seek Me, even so do I respond to them; for all men follow My path in every way.'

— **Lord Krishna**

Bhagavad Gita, Chapter 4 Verse 11

Meera Bai
Pure Devotional Love Prema Bhakti

Meera Bai sought and reached Lord Krishna with Prema Bhakti (Divine Love). She in her life on earth met Lord Krishna few times as Krishna will reveal Himself when sought with love and devotion. He is always around. Only devotion is able to see. Meera is an exceptional reference of highest sacrifice because of deepest devotional love. She is source of great inspiration on the path of Prema Bhakti.

Meera Bai spent her whole life loving and seeking Lord Krishna. She is a motivation and inspiration for Krishna lovers. Meera was a devotional poetess as she sang devotional love songs in praise of Lord Krishna.

Meera Bai was born in 1499 A.D in Rajasthan. She was daughter of a King. Her parents were great devotees of Lord Vishnu. She was brought up as a normal Princess and was taught Scriptures, Music, horse riding, skills for war but she fell in love with Lord Krishna at the age of 4.

She, along with her mother, at the age of four was watching a marriage procession when she enquired from her mother about the marriage procession. She asked her mother as to who will be her bridegroom.

Her mother said to the innocent child 'Lord Krishna is your love and He will marry you.' She was given an idol of Lord Krishna by her mother. It is also mentioned that she received the idol of Lord Krishna from Raidas (Ravidas) ji who was Meera's Guru and mentor. She lived day and night with that idol, dressed the idol, decorated the idol and sung beautiful songs and danced in front of the Krishna idol.

Rana Sangha, King of Mewar, had a son by the name Rana Kumbha. They heard of Meera's devotional love and pious nature. Rana Sangha approached Rao Duda (Grandfather of Meera) who had brought up Meera with lot of love and care.

Rao Duda accepted the marriage proposal but Meera did not want to marry as she felt that she was already surrendered to Lord Krishna and could not think of any Human Being as her husband. But she could not say no to her Grandfather Rao Duda. It is also believed that she had a dream from Lord Krishna that she should accept the marriage proposal as she needs to perform her duty and she can reach Lord Krishna while performing her duty as was done by Gopis in Vrindavan. She accepted the proposal and she was married to Rana Kumbha in 1513 when she was just 13 years old and she moved to Mewar after her marriage.

As ordained, Meera was dutiful. She left for Mewar with Rana Kumbha. She obeyed her husband's commands. Scholars maintain that Rana was a great devotee of the Lord Himself, and wrote the treatise known as 'Rasipriya' and a grammatical work 'SangItarajam' on the immortal work of Jayadeva Goswami and Geet Govindam. He had sought Meera's hand out of admiration for her devotion and love to the Lord, which he felt he too shared.

One historical version of Meera's life states that the Rana Kumbha died in a battle within ten years of their marriage, as did her sympathetic father-in-law Rana Sangha (who named Meera his successor before dying). At this juncture, the Rana's relatives began persecuting Meera in various ways, even though Meera had no desire for the throne. The tortures and torments came from the brother and successor of Kumbha Rana (Meera's late husband) and his cousin sister Udabai. It was no different from what Prahlada was subjected to by his father Hiranyakashipu. Hari shielded Prahlada.

Here, Krishna always stood by Meera. Meera was sent a basket with a cobra inside and a message that the basket contained a garland of flowers. Meera, after meditation, opened the basket and found inside a lovely idol of Sri Krishna with a garland of flowers. The relentless Rana (her brother-in-law) sent her a cup of poison with the message that it was nectar. Meera offered it to her Lord Krishna and took it as His Prasad. It was real nectar to her. The bed of nails that the Rana sent transformed into a bed of roses when Meera reposed on it.

The other version about what happened to Rana (Meera's husband and King) is one where the Rana outlives (survives) Meera. In this version, the confused Rana turned a deaf ear through Meera's trials and tribulations at the hands of his conniving relatives; however, he became heartbroken upon Meera's departure from Mewar.

It is believed that the turning point in Meera's life (which precipitated her departure from Mewar and hence her earthly bonds) occurred when once Akbar and his court musician Tansen came in disguise to Chitore to hear Meera's devotional and inspiring songs. Both entered the temple and listened to Meera's soul-stirring songs to their heart's content. Akbar was really moved. Before he departed, he touched the holy feet of Meera and placed a necklace of priceless gems in front of the idol as a present. Somehow the news reached the Rana Kumbha that Akbar had entered the sacred temple in disguise, touched the feet of Meera and even presented her a necklace. The Rana became furious. He told Meera, "Drown yourself in the river and never show your face to the world in future. You have brought great disgrace on my family".

Meera obeyed the words of her husband and King. She proceeded to the river to drown herself. The names of the Lord *"Govinda, Giridhari, Gopala"* were always on her lips. She sang and danced in ecstasy on her way to the river. When she raised her feet from the ground, a hand from behind grasped her and embraced her. She turned behind and saw her beloved Giridhari. She fainted on Him. After a few minutes she opened her eyes. Lord Krishna smiled and gently whispered: "My dear Meera, your life with your mortal relatives is over now. You are absolutely free. Be cheerful. You are and have always been mine. Proceed immediately to the bowers of Vraja and the avenues of Vrindavan. Seek Me there, my dear. Start now".

Meera walked barefoot on the hot sandy beds of Rajasthan. On her way, many ladies, children and devotees received her with great hospitality. She reached Vrindavan. She reached the Chitchor Gopala. It was at Brindavan that she again met and was inspired by Sant Raidas. She went about Brindavan doing *Oonchavritti* and worshipped in the *Govinda Mandir*, which has since become famous and is now a great place of pilgrimage for devotees from all over the world. Her devotees of Chitore came to Brindavan to see Meera. A repentant Kumbha came to Vrindavan to see Meera in the disguise of a mendicant, revealed Himself and prayed that he may be forgiven for all his previous wrongs and cruel deeds. He begged that Meera return to the kingdom and assumed her role as the queen once more. Meera at once prostrated before her husband, and gently added, 'What is Kulam or lineage, heritage or inheritance? What is the meaning of the division amongst devotees as Kshatriyas and Brahmanas and shudras and the like? Who is man and who is woman? Krishna is the only Purusha and all of us are women. He is Pati and we are all Pasus. I am no more Queen than you are King. There is only one King and my life belongs to him.' Kumbha reminisced for a moment of the days when he wrote the treatises on Gita Govindam and how he had desired the hand of the finest lady of his times for spiritual reasons. His eyes welled up when he was forcibly taken to his dark days of jealousy, rancour and the torture he inflicted on the great soul of divine import. The KumbhaRana, for the first time, truly understood Meera's exalted state of mind and prostrated before her in reverence. He then promptly left Vrindavan a changed soul.

Jiva Gosain was the head of the Vaishnavites in Brindavan. Meera wanted to have Darshan of Jiva Gosain. He declined to see her. He sent word to Meera that he would not allow any woman in his presence. Meera Bai retorted: «Everybody in Brindavan is a woman. Only Giridhar Gopala is Purusha. Today only I have come to know that there is another Purusha besides Krishna in Brindavan». He felt that Meera was indeed a *paramabhaktha* or the supreme devotee of the Lord. He at once went to see Meera and paid her due respects.

Meera's fame spread far and wide. She was immersed in *satsang* day in and out. At the request of Rana Kumbha, Meera returned to Mewar and Kumbha agreed to her request that she would reside in the temple of Krishna but would not restrict her movements and wanderings. From Mewar, she once again returned to Brindavan, and then went on to Dwaraka. The King went with her. Dwaraka was to be the place where her Gopala would take her unto Him at the temple of Ranchod.

There are, once again, two versions to Meera's union with her Supreme Lord. In one version, the following took place on Krishna's Janamashtami at the temple of Ranchodi (Krishna). There was much happiness all around in the abode of the Lord. The light of the lamps, the sound of the bhajans and the energy from the devotees' ecstasy were filling the air.

With Tamburi in one hand and cymbals or *chipla* in the other the great *tapasvini* was singing ecstatically with her Gopala smiling in front of her closed eyes. Meera stood up and danced with her song '*Mere Janama Marana ke sathee*', and when the song ended, Kumbha gently approached her and requested her to come back. Meera said, 'Ranaji, the body is yours and you are a great devotee, but my mind, emotions and the soul are all HIS. I do not know what use am I to you at this state of mind'.

Kumbha was moved and he started singing with her in unison. Meera rose up abruptly, stumbled and fell at the flowers on the feet of Giridhari. 'Oh, Giridhari, are you calling me, I am coming'. When Kumbha and the rest were watching in awe, there was a lightning which enveloped Meera and the sanctum doors closed on their own. When the doors opened again, Meera's saree was enveloping Lord Krishna's idol and her voice and the flute accompaniment were the only sounds that could be heard.

In the second version, Meera was invited back to Mewar by the Rana just as she had reached Dwaraka. Reluctant to leave her Krishna, Meera asked permission to spend the night at the temple of Ranchhorji. The next morning her lifeless body was found lying at His feet. It is believed that her spirit entered the deity during the night.

Historians and scholars put this date at 1546 A.D.

Meerabai was a devotional poetess and wrote hundreds of songs that have been sung by many singers. Meerabai looked upon Lord Krishna to love her and accept her like Lord loved Radha. Her song below reflects her respect for Radha and Krishna.

Jo Tum Chhoodo Piya, Main Nahi Chhodu re ...

Jo tum chhoodo piya
Main nahi chhodu re
Tosai preet joudi Krishna
Kaun sang joudu re…
    Meera nai toe keh daala,
    Main kya boolu mere Ram,
    Is kalyug ke bhoolbhlaiya mein khoye
    Mere who sawarai, sunder Shyam
Janam sai he, iss vyakkol mann mein,
Ek pyaas ajeeb samayee hai
Mein bhi banoo ek din piya ki pyaree
Yeh tujhe se duhai hai
    Itna toe batla de o Bhagwan
    Is bhanwar mein jo tune utaara hai
    Mere Kanha ko bhi is kalyug mein
    Behshaque tone kahin banaaya hai
Mann main bassi hai moore Prabhu
Meera ki he madhoor vani,
Tann mein agann jale hai morai
Radha se mai prem diwanee
    Iss matwali kaari duniya mein
    Morai Kaanha, tohe kahan dhoondhu mai,
    Mein tori raah ektook ho dekhoo
    Bus aur kuch bhi naa janoo mai
Pal bhi yeh aass nahi mitt-paatee
Ke ek din tu bhi aayeega,
Is bawari, akeli bairagan ko he
Tu saprem apni Radha banayega

We will share a beautiful story narrated by Pandit ji from Vaishno Devi during the evening prayers of Mata Vaishno Devi.

Narada ji came to earth. A devotee sitting on the banks of river Ganges requested Narada ji that when he meets Lord Vishnu, please ask when will I get to see Him. Little later another devotee sitting in devotion under a holy tree put up the same request to Narada ji.

When Narada ji met Lord Krishna, Lord Krishna said that tell the Devotee that I will meet Him after he spends 5 more births in meditation, and to the other that he should count the number of leaves on the tree and I will meet Him after he spends so many births in devotion. Narada ji went to the person sitting on river Ganges and when told him that Vishnu will meet him after he has taken 5 more births, he got angry. In anger he broke his chanting beads and ran after Narada ji. Somehow, Narada ji managed to escape. Now he was worried as to what will happen when I tell the devotee sitting under the holy tree that he needs to take as many births as leaves on the tree before he can meet Hari.

When Devotee saw Narada ji, he ran towards Narada ji to meet him but Narada ji asked him to keep distance. He told Him what Lord Krishna told him and ran towards the opposite direction. But when he did not see him following, he looked back and saw that devotee was jumping in joy that Lord Krishna will meet him. Narada ji came close to watching him singing and dancing in joy. He had no worry after how many births but was joyful that Lord Krishna will meet him. He became so absorbed in that joy that he fell down on ground with heads down but as he was about to hit the ground, Narada ji saw that he fell in Lord Krishna's lap.

Narada ji bowed down to Lord Hari and asked what happened. Lord Krishna said that I cannot see my true devotee falling down.

'Your right is to work only and never to the fruit thereof. Do not consider yourself to be the cause of the fruit of action; nor let your attachment to be to inaction'

— Lord Krishna

Bhagavad Gita, Chapter 2 Verse 47

Faith in Him

This verse is for every Human being irrespective of his Natural Duties. What it conveys is that there is a system that is watching you. That system is much more powerful than this Human developed system. If you are not on the right track, that system will catch up with you. It is powerful enough to take away this Human birth from yourself and put you in the lower worlds of insects and animals and it is powerful enough that it can take you to God's home above Time.

When that system is watching you with thousand eyes, you do not need to worry about any other system if you are on the righteous path and you have no escape from that system if you are not on the right path. That system knows how to catch up with you.

'All perishable objects are Adhibhuta; the shining Purusa (Brahma) is Adhidaiva; and in this body I Myself, dwelling as the inner witness, am Adhiyajna, O Arjuna'

— **Lord Krishna**

Bhagavad Gita, Chapter 8 Verse 4

Lord is saying, 'I am Adhiyajna'. I am sitting inside you as witness. Not only your soul which is complete God is witness to everything we do, here Lord says that His own presence in each Soul is there as a witness. Lord is Himself Witness to everything we do and everything everyone else does and He has a system to deal with everything, This is also a reason that Lord is saying that focus on your Karmas and Actions. Do not worry to run His system or interfere in His system. His system is watching everyone and will reward/punish every act. Lord explaining about the supreme power further affirms;

'It has hands and feet on all sides, eyes, head and mouth in all directions, and ears all–around; for it stands pervading all in the universe.'

— **Lord Krishna**

Bhagavad Gita, Chapter 13 Verse 13

Lord further confirms that he is watching every activity of ours. He is listening to everything we say. He is analyzing every thought of ours. He has hands and feet to deal with us whenever he wishes.

' The Spirit dwelling in this body, is really same as the Supreme. He has been spoken of as the Witness, the true Guide, the Sustainer of all, the Experiencer (as the embodied soul), the Overlord and the Absolute as well.

— **Lord Krishna**

Bhagavad Gita, Chapter 13 Verse 22

Our soul is the same as Supreme which means the soul in the people with whom you deal is also same as Supreme. So be cautious of how you deal, how you speak and how you perform in His universe and His environment. He is the witness to everything we do – so our own soul is witness which is Supreme. He is also Adhiyajana and is sitting inside us as a witness. He is a true Guide so if we listen to Him, He will guide us on the righteous path. He is sustaining everyone. He is Oversoul and He is Absolute.

'Arjuna; Poor and wretched are those who are the cause in making their actions bear fruit'.

— Lord Krishna

Bhagavad Gita, Chapter 2 Verse 49

When you make your actions bear fruit, you forget that there is another system that is working to get you fruits as per your actions. Your entire attention goes to worldly desires and you are lost in the spiritual journey. When you do everything right and have faith in His system, then you know His system is watching and will do the justice. This is also natural, the one who runs this universe and brings forward the multitude of beings according to their Karmas is watching you every moment with thousand eyes, so you do not need to influence His creation to get the results in your favour, leave it to Him and His system to decide the results. An individual is although advised during *Bhagavad Gita* to just stay focused on Individual's natural duties and actions.

Meera Bai has sung a beautiful Bhajan on Karma and how our Karma writes Destiny:

Rama Kahiye, Govind Kahiye
karam ki gati nyaari santo
bade bade nayan diye miragan ko
ban ban phirat ughaari santo
karam ki gati nyaari santo
ujjawal varan dinhi bagalan ko

Faith in Him

koyal kar dinhi kaari santo
karam ki gati nyaari santo
auran dipan jal nirmal kinhi
samundar karatini khaari santo
karam ki gati nyaari santo
murakh ko tum raaj diyat ho
pandit phirat bhikhaari santo
karam ki gati nyaari santo
meera ke prabhu giridhar naagun
raja ji to kaun bichaari santo

Bhaktidevi Tulasi Maharani

Vrinda, a devotee of Lord Vishnu, became a Tulasi plant which is worshipped in every Hindu Family. Tulasi leaves should be offered to Lord Krishna every day. Lord accepts offerings with love when we place a Tulasi leaf on the offerings/Prasadam. Tulasi worshipping gives the blessing for Krishna Bhakti. In Hindu homes, devotees light a lamp with Tulasi plant every night. Tulasi worshipped Lord Hari all her life and sacrificed her life in devotion to Lord. Her real name is Vrinda. Vrindavan is named after Vrinda where Radha-Krishna resided.

It is believed that God's Home above Time is also Vrindavan.

"Every home with a Tulasi plant is a place of pilgrimage, and no diseases, messengers of Yama, the God of Death, can enter it." *Skandapurana 2, 4, 8, 13 Padmapurana Uttarakhanda*

"Wherever the aroma of Tulasi is carried by the wind, it purifies the atmosphere and frees all animals from all baser tendencies." *Padmapurana, Uttarakhanda*

"Vishnu, the Lord of the Three Worlds, takes up abode in the village or the house where Tulasi is grown. In such a house no one suffers calamities like poverty, illness or separations from dear ones." *Padmapurana, Uttarakhanda, 6-24-31-32*

Tulasi Prayer

Asta-Nama-Stava from the Padma Purana - The Eight Names of Vrinda-devi.

Vrindavani, Vrinda, visvapujita, pushpasara, nandini, Krishna-jivani, visva-pavani, tulasi.

- VRINDAVANI – One who first manifested in Vrindavan.

- **VRINDA-** the goddess of all plant and trees (even if one Tulasi plant is present in a forest it can be called Vrindavana.)
- **VISHVAPUJITA** – One whom the whole universe worships.
- **PUSHPASARA-** the topmost of all flowers, without whom Krishna does not like to look upon the flowers
- **NANDINI** – Seeing whom gives unlimited bliss to the devotees
- **KRISHNA-JIVANI** – the life of Sri Krishna
- **VISHVA-PAVANI** – One who purifies the three worlds.
- **TULASI** – One who has no comparison.

Anyone while worshipping Tulasi-devi chants these eight names will get the same results as one who performs the Ashvamedha sacrifices. And one who on the full-moon day of Kartika (Tulasi-devi's appearance day) worships Her with this Mantra will break free from the bonds of this miserable world of birth and death, and very quickly attains Goloka Vrindavan.

On the full moon-day of Kartik lord Sri Krishna Himself worships Srimati Tulasi-devi with this Mantra.

One who remembers this Mantra will very quickly attain devotion to Lord Krishna's Transcedental Lotus Feet.

Tulasi is the life of Krsna and She gives unlimited bliss to the devotees. She is the best of all the flowers and Her presence is required on any garland to be worn by Krsna. She is one who has no comparison. Tulasi purifies the three worlds and is worshiped all over the universe. Tulasi is the goddess of all plants and trees and She first manifested in Vrindavana. (Padam Purana)

Sri Tulasi-kirtana

1
namo namah tulasi! krsna-preyasi
radha-krsna-seva pabo ei abhilasi

2
je tomara sarana loy, tara vancha purna hoy
krpa kori' koro tare brndavana-basi

3
mor ei abhilas, bilas kunje dio vas
nayane heribo sada jugala-rupa-rasi

4
ei nivedana dharo, sakhir anugata koro
seva-adhikara diye koro nija dasi

5
dina krsna-dase koy, ei jena mora hoy
sri-radha-govinda-preme sada jena bhasi

(1) O Tulasi, beloved of Krsna, I bow before you again and again. My desire is to obtain the service of Sri Sri Radha-Krsna.

(2) Whoever takes shelter of you has his wishes fulfilled. Bestowing your mercy on him, you make him a resident of Vrndavana.

(3) My desire is that you will also grant me a residence in the pleasure groves of Sri Vrndavana-dhama. Thus, within my vision I will always behold the beautiful pastimes of Radha and Krsna.

(4) I beg you to make me a follower of the cowherd damsels of Vraja. Please give me the privilege of devotional service and make me your own maidservant.

(5) This very fallen and lowly servant of Krsna prays, "May I always swim in the love of Sri Radha and Govinda.

Tulasi-devi once cursed Lord Hari and converted Lord to stone. We worship that form of Lord as Shaligram. This was power of a devotee. This power was drawn from Lord Krishna. So Tulasi also used Vishnu's power to curse Lord Vishnu. Now this is the power of love. You cannot love God as much as God can love you, truly so because Lord is a creator of love.

Lord Krishna is the form of Shaligram and Tulasi marriage is performed in the month of Kartik from Ekadshi to Purnima (Full Moon day)

When Tulasi cursed Lord Hari and Lord became a stone (worshipped as Shaligram in that form), there was restlessness all over the universe as everyone drew power from Lord Krishna. So Lord Shiva came to Tulasi to ask to free up Lord from the curse and Tulasi did it but she disappeared in her Vrinda form and appeared as Tulasi.

Tulasi was blessed by Lord Shiva that she will be worshipped as wife of Lord Krishna and she will always be unmarried.

The *Tulabharam* is an incident that reveals the extent to which humble devotion is worth more than material wealth.

Satyabhama, wife of Lord Krishna, once observed Vrata (Fast) for Krishna. When she completed her fast, she was to give Gold and Ornaments equal to the weight of Lord Krishna to Narada ji. On the final day, Lord Krishna sat on one side of the scale and loads of Gold Ornaments were loaded on the other side of the scale but with all the available Gold and Ornaments, Lord could not be lifted.

This made Satyabhama very nervous as she was to give that offering to Narada ji. Narada ji asked Satyabhama to take help from Krishna's eldest wife Rukmini. She placed a Tulasi leaf on the ornaments and scale moved up and Lord Krishna got lifted. To further prove the respect Lord Krishna had for Tulasi, all the gold ornaments were removed and still the Tulasi leaf could lift Lord Krishna.

Lord Krishna is creator of the universe and all the worlds from Brahmlok reside in Lord Krishna. Lord Krishna is on one side of the balance and a Tulasi leaf is on the other side of the balance. Lord got lifted. This was power of love and sacrifice as Lord says that 'As people worship me so do I respond to them'.

Love will get responded with love. Material desire will get responded with fulfilment of material gains.

Mother Sita, wife of Shri Rama was serving food to Hanuman ji. Hanuman ji was eating and asking to serve more. No food was left and Hanuman ji was still hungry asking for food. Shri Rama (Lord Krishna and Lord Rama are same Gods) asked for a Tulasi leaf to be served to Hanuman ji and Hanuman ji felt his stomach was full.

Tulasi water is sprinkled for purification. It is a belief that where Tulasi lives, no bad omen can happen.

Journey of a God-realised Soul

God Realised Souls take on the following to complete the journey to their home within this birth.

1. **Sattva Life** – Food, Behaviour (Nature), Actions, type of Sacrifice. This makes the foundation for the journey very strong. If Sattva life is not started, one is bound to fall somewhere in the journey, most likely right in the beginning and may not go far.
2. **Meditation** – Brings in the pull from God's side and keeps us on the track for God's Home. God says that among Yagyas, I am Jaap Yagya so He is always there with you when you meditate. He is there with you as an eternal guide.
3. **Sacrifice** – Helps erase the past sins and makes you Humble that helps you in advancing the journey. Fasting helps in the purification process. Krishna devotees observe Ekadshi Fast.
4. **Renunciation** – This can also be termed as Dispassion. Without renunciation which is the final step, reaching His home is not possible. Why this is important is that till you have dispassion, you have passion for something other than Him and He is going to help you get whatever is your wish. This works as a major obstacle for the blessed in their final step to journey to His home.

Lord says – One in thousands starts His eternal journey. That one in thousands listens to the eternal voice and starts this journey by listening to the science of soul like *Bhagavad Gita*. This one in thousands is a deserving one who has purified himself or has concluded that there is nothing else but God. Now this one in thousand is a blessed soul.

Among these blessed souls who are all on the righteous path and do not do any mistake, only one in thousands make to His home like King Janak, Meera, Tulsi, like Prahlad.

Who is the one in these thousand blessed souls that make to His home—they are the ones who got into dispassion with Sattva life. Other blessed ones get their wishes fulfilled and are satisfied. They get what they want and they continue meditating, continue following a Sattva life, continue sacrifices but also continue enjoying the material blessings.

There is a big difference between material blessings and spiritual blessings. Meera was daughter of a king and wife of a king. Tulasi (Vrinda) had all pleasures to her disposal. King Janaka was a born king; Prahlada was a Prince but none of them felt satisfied with the material blessings as they felt spiritual blessings were way above. They wanted Lord Krishna. They found Him through dispassion and love for Him alone. Gopis never aspired for any material gain.

When you start the Sattva journey with meditation and sacrifice, you become one of the thousands that start the journey towards Him and when you are blessed and you aspire for material gains, you become one of the blessed ones who do not make to His home. Only one of the thousand blessed ones who has observed Dispassion and Renunciation makes it to His home.

Sattva Life

Sattva life means food habits that are inclined towards natural food that offers a healthy feeling in Individuals. One is truthful and humble and is not hurting anyone.

There is a beautiful verse in *Bhagavad Gita* that covers the start and end of the journey. It has an extremely deep meaning. *Bhagavad Gita* is full of depth.

'He who is not a source of annoyance to his fellow creatures, and who in his turn does not feel vexed with his fellow creatures, and who is free from delight and envy, perturbation and fear is dear to me.'

— **Lord Krishna**

Bhagavad Gita, Chapter 12 Verse 15

Lord says that one who is not a source of annoyance to his fellow beings means one who is not hurting anyone. One who adopts Sattva habits will not hurt anyone. He will be a person who is liked by everyone. Sattva habits are start of the journey. Then lord says—who in his turn does not feel vexed with his fellow creatures. This is something one will have in his nature when one has reached an advanced stage of meditation and renunciation. He will not feel hurt by anyone. He will take another person's behaviour in his stride. No one can disturb his peace of mind. No one can take away his attention from Lord Krishna. He is not disturbed. He does not deviate from the path and does not waste time in petty things and instead advances on his journey.

This one is difficult to achieve but will become easy as the journey advances. When one is sitting hundred miles away, one will feel the distance is long but as you keep progressing and stay focused on the next few miles, destinations look nearer and easier. So, these feelings will naturally come in as one advances on the journey.

Lord further says that one who is free from delight and envy, perturbation and fear is dear to me. This means that the person has reached dispassion. He is all set to cover the last miles. Journey becomes easier as one advances because the pull working from His home becomes stronger. One has to initially work hard to get out of the pull of the material world. When the pull from the material world is strong, then the pull from His home goes weak. Initial discomforts and hardships return the everlasting happiness in results.

Sacrifice

Sacrifice means doing something for a good cause with no expectation of returns like feeding the poor and seeing it as a natural duty as God has gifted you with all life's necessities You feel that God has showered enough blessings and you ought to share it with deserving people. Like, parents sacrifice for their children by staying awake in the night to take care of the little ones, when parents work hard to earn so that they can give good food, shelter and education to their children. They love them as God's gift and take this as their natural duty.

Fasting for God on specific days is a Sacrifice. Lord Krishna has mentioned that reading *Bhagavad Gita* is a sacrifice of the wisdom.

'The man who listens to the holy Gita with reverence, being free from malice, he too, liberated from sin, shall reach the propitious worlds of the virtuous'

— **Lord Krishna**

Bhagavad Gita, Chapter 18 Verse 71

Sacrifice performed for a good cause with no eye on the return or keeping no expectation purifies the individual.

'Man is bound by his own action except when it is performed for the sake of sacrifice. Therefore, Arjuna, do you efficiently perform your duty, free from attachment for the sake of sacrifice alone.'

— **Lord Krishna**

Bhagavad Gita, Chapter 3 Verse 9

Lord asked Arjuna to perform his natural duty of a religious warrior for the sake of sacrifice with no eye on the result of the war. He advised that this sacrifice is for a religious cause. All natural duties when performed with no eye on return are sacrifices. The same duties when performed with an eye on return are bindings. So, when we bring up the children with an expectation that we will get something in return from them, then the sacrifice has taken a different shape. When you perform sacrifice, you are not bound by your actions and that is dispassion and that is the journey to His home.

Life is a constant journey, every day we get up and we move in some direction. Some keep moving every day towards His home by doing everything right. Some keep moving away from Him every day by doing everything wrong. Some do mixed actions and take few steps in every direction weaving a thread towards all corners and then getting entangled in the same thread. That is why it is so important to watch your actions every day as the journey is continuing every day. No one is going to make a jump in the last days to His home unless there is a healthy support of Karmas (good Actions), meditation, purification by sacrifice and dispassion.

'Arjuna, Yogis who enjoy the nectar that has been left over after the performance of a sacrifice attain the eternal Brahma. To the man who does not offer sacrifice, even this world is not happy; how, then, can the other world be happy?'

— **Lord Krishna**

Bhagavad Gita, Chapter 4 Verse 31

Yogis who enjoy the eternal nectar after the sacrifice are absolved of all sins as you perform all actions for Him. He is present everywhere; it is a matter of recognizing and seeing Him. Sun cannot shine without Him; flowers will not blossom without Him.

Human birth is a big blessing as it gives you the insight for God realization and an opportunity to advance on a journey towards God and reach His home within this birth. Karmas are not allowed in lower worlds births and these births are there for a defined period depending on the karmas. Higher worlds of heaven also do not allow new karmas as that is a place for enjoyment of the fruits of good actions and to exhaust the merits. Human birth is the only birth where one can perform new Karmas, sacrifice, natural duties and then reach His home is this Human birth. Scriptures deeply cover the value of this birth and advise to watch your actions. Lord Krishna towards the end of *Bhagavad Gita* advised Arjuna that this is a very rare and blessed birth and you should not lose any moment when you are not advancing on your journey towards God realization.

Arjuna had to perform his karmas for God realization. He was living with God day and night. God was driving his chariot in the battlefield. He had such a proximity to God that even Meera, Vrinda, Prahalad did not have. He lived his entire life with Him but still God advised to reach Him through righteous Karmas and did not take Him along.

And it is right when Lord says that He is working all the time else He will become the reason for destruction of all the worlds as all the worlds draw inspiration from Him. While he has nothing to achieve, He still keeps working. So, it is a natural phenomenon that everyone has to perform their natural duties and reach Him through the righteous Karmas.

Sacrifice and Meditation leads to purification. Purification leads to good nature and good karmas. It will not be right to ignore or waste God's blessing on us with this Human birth and material richness.

'The virtuous who partake of what is left over after sacrifice, are absolved of all sins. Those sinful ones who cook for the sake of nourishing their bodies alone, partake of sin only.'

— **Lord Krishna**

Bhagavad Gita, Chapter 3 Verse 13

Living life without sacrifice is living a sinful life.

Man is bound by his own actions other than the actions performed for the sake of sacrifice. When you do positive actions, you get to reap good results of positive actions. When you perform negative actions, you get to reap the punishments of negative actions—His rules are always perfect and they work accordingly. So binding exists either way—in positive actions and in negative actions.

Skill lies in in-action which is not practical or you perform all actions and dedicate all actions to Him. When you do that, you do not get to reap the results of the actions. This is surrender. This is the path to His home.

When you dedicate actions to Him, your actions cannot be negative. So you perform actions which are Sattvika and then dedicate to Him. Sacrifice is actions dedicated to Lord.

Bhagavad Gita was revealed in a battlefield when Arjuna refused to fight the righteous war. That is when Lord Krishna reminded him on the importance of the righteous karmas in the spiritual journey.

Importance should be attached to the word 'Righteous'. We all perform actions as we cannot live without performing actions. What we need to see is that are we performing the right actions (in our natural duties) as per scriptures or as per the rules of this material world. Either way we are on a journey and the journey cannot stop. The journey has to continue.

Natural Duties are duties by birth. When the birth happened, it was a continuity of a previous journey. Arjuna was a warrior. He was in the battlefield and he was fighting a religious war for the right. Lord advised him that for a person born in a warrior class who is doing his duty to protect the right in a battlefield,, it is a righteous Karma and no sin will accrue for performing that action. Rather it is your natural duty and must be performed. Also Krishna told Arjuna that this was an unsolicited war.

Natural Duties for those in business and jobs are again righteous actions that are based on truthfulness, trust in relationships, no cheating, keeping in mind that His system is watching.

Take the life of a housewife. You are gifted with lot of money and a big family. Your natural duties as housewife are taking good care of children and elders, giving everyone the love and care they need. Your natural duty is to put children on a righteous path, on a spiritual path, so that they advance journey towards God and not to put them on a material track where they are lost. Money has lot of power in the material world with no recognition in the spiritual world if it deviates its purpose as per the scriptures. So your money has to be a facilitator for you to advance your journey towards the spiritual world and it should not prove to be a hindrance or inhibitor. If it is serving the purpose of helping to advance the journey because you do work for charity, you sacrifice, you fast then this is a blessing that is helping you to advance in the journey. If the same money puts the children on an arrogance track and they adopt *Tamasika* habits then the same money becomes a curse. If you become the source of inspiration to the children to advance in the spiritual journey, then the real purpose of life is well met. If you fail to inspire your children, then they become a source of nuisance to the world and you are responsible for their journey away from God. Then you cannot run away when you have been failed as influencers.

His system is watching our acts and will not leave us. Also, if you run the whole system with money giving no care to other things, you will find that in your old age this system will start working against you. You will find that children have advanced so much in the material world and material journey even if they do not do anything wrong that they had no time for you and did not care for you. The source of all this is no one but ourselves. Here we have hurt ourselves because we do not have anyone caring for us and we are further getting blamed in the spiritual system that we have put many souls on a wrong path. We cannot wash off our hands by saying that this is their own doing, they looked up at us on what they should do. They tried to follow us.

When they became adults, they got influenced by the society but their raw years were with us. If they are ruined on the spiritual path, we got to be questioned. If they do not take care of us personally rather help us monetarily only then this system was developed by us. His system is watching us with thousand eyes, our soul is recording every act we do. His system will not support us when we ask for support as His system will see us as the source of all confusion.

Now, let's take another side. You are a housewife and you are gifted with all luxuries money can get you. You decide to teach children moral values. You teach them everything towards the spiritual path. You perform sacrifices for the family; you take care of elders with genuine care from the heart. You sacrifice your time and energy in giving love and care to the children and be their friend at every step ensuring that they move towards the spiritual path (what they call in religious language as *Sanskara*).

Now when you hit old age, try taking no support from them and go through the old age sufferings and pains all by yourself. You will miserably fail in doing this because His system has thousand eyes and He watched you through the upbringing process of the children. Children will not leave you, they will take care of every bit of your need. They make sure that even if you try to shun them or try to move away from them, they will not let you do that. Sanskaras have been instilled in their blood and soul. Your wish of staying away and not getting care will neither get heard by children nor by His system.

'It is action without attachment alone that Janaka and other wise men reached perfection. Having in view the maintenance of the world order too, you should take to action'

— **Lord Krishna**

Bhagavad Gita, Chapter 3 Verse 20

King Janaka has been referenced in *Bhagavad Gita* as having got the perfection as a Karmayogi even while he was living the life of a King and a household person. King Janaka ruled the complete Kingdom in a sattvika manner but what made king perfect was detachment and renunciation while living the life of a King. He dedicated every action to God while staying on a righteous path. *Bhagavad Gita* references that if a King who has everything under him can live a renounced and detached life, why can others not live like him?

Now God also talks of 'maintenance of the world order', which means that the King was expected to live like a King and not like any other person. Similarly, if one is a rich person, he does not need to lead a life where he gets noticed on an unnatural behaviour. He should live a normal life like a royal person leads. He should have a Home where God will love to come, His behaviour should be loved by everyone. He should not be a nuisance but an enabler to put more people on God's path and also his richness should become a source of food for deserving. So God advises to keep the Maintenance of the world order and just behave naturally with your level following sacrifices, meditation and dispassion.

While talking of King Janaka, I remember a beautiful story in 'Sukh Sagar'. There are 4 yugas—*Satyuga, Tretayuga, Dwaparyuga* and *Kaliyuga*. Satyuga is when everyone leads a very religious life and then over the period, it deteriorates to Kaliyuga where religion has very limited presence with few people.

In Satyuga, the purity is at the highest level. Kings rule the kingdom in a righteous manner. Earth gives food even without doing agriculture, rains come on time and so on. Because of purity, Human beings are able to see God's people who come to earth to receive the souls after the death of Human Beings.

Now many scriptures talk about Death that it happens at a defined time, defined place with a defined reason so it is pre-written and God's people come to the place before time and wait for the person to die with the right reason. There has been a belief that if one can somehow defeat one of the above, he can defeat God's system for a while but then no one has ever been successful.

So, the story (real happening) goes like this. King Janaka had a minister who overheard God's people on earth talking to each other and they were talking about the Minister's death the same day evening. The Minister immediately went to King Janaka and told him about what he heard and asked for a favour to take the best horse from the King's palace so that he could go far away from that place. King Janaka gave his consent. In those days the fastest mode of journey was horses. So, the Minister had covered few hundred miles before the evening.

Next day, King Janaka heard God's people talking to each other saying that they saw the Minister the previous morning near the king's palace, while his death was written to happen the same evening many hundred miles away. They were wondering that the minister would not die because he was at the palace and death was written hundreds of miles away. So, the Minister had actually gone to the place of his death.

'Arjuna, he who does not follow the wheel of creation thus set going in this world, i.e. does not perform his duties, leads a sinful and sensual life, he lives in vain'

— **Lord Krishna**

Bhagavad Gita, Chapter 3 Verse 16

Natural duties must be performed. Natural duties will be pleasant and unpleasant but these are natural duties. But the one who keeps offering and performs all his actions to God, gets rid of the results. Hence, the skill is in action and dedicating all actions to Him and considering self as the non-doer. When all actions are dedicated to Him, you will never go wrong and you will be blessed. The destination will be His home because the Good actions do not take you to Heaven as these have been offered to Him and the actions that do not produce pleasant results (performed consciously or ignorantly) also do not produce any sin as all actions have been offered to Him.

Hence Lord Krishna asked Arjuna to dedicate and offer all his actions to God.

This also brings in His constant remembrance and Lord Krishna says that one who remembers me at the time of Death undoubtedly comes to me but one will remember Him at the time of death only if one has been remembering Him all his life.

'Arjuna, there is no duty in all the three worlds for Me to perform nor is there anything worth attaining, unattained by Me., yet I continue to work'

— Lord Krishna

Bhagavad Gita, Chapter 3 Verse 22

Lord has to work all the Time because souls inside us are connected to Lord all the time. Some rare people have that consciousness. If the oversoul stops working, then all the planets like Sun, Moon, Earth and our souls that draw energy from Him will be lost. Unconsciously souls will get the inspiration that oversoul is not in action, so the souls too will go out of action. Lord Krishna said in *Bhagavad Gita* that if He decides not to work, then the whole universe will be lost and He will become the cause for this confusion.

Ekadshi Fast

Ekadhshi falls on the 11th day when the moon is rising and on the 11th day when moon is diminishing. Krishna devotees observe fast on Ekadshi. Ekadshi is Goddess that emerged out of Lord Vishnu.

Lord Vishnu fought with a demon for many years but could not defeat him. So Lord wanted to take some rest. While Lord was sleeping, demon wanted to attack Lord. At that time a Goddess emerged from Lord Vishnu, and fought and killed the demon.

When Lord Vishnu got up, he saw the demon was dead and a Goddess was praying to Lord Vishnu with folded hands. Lord asked who killed the demon and who the Goddess was.

She said that she killed the demon and she was His own internal power that emerged from Him when the demon was trying to attack Lord in His sleep.

Lord Vishnu named the Goddess as Ekadshi as she appeared on Ekadshi day and blessed her and said that Ekadshi date will be most dear to the Lord.

Krishna devotees observe Ekadshi fast as this brings in showers of blessings from Lord Krishna.

Meditation

There is a vicious circle. Nature influences Karmas and Karmas decide destiny. So, when the nature is not friendly, then you are unable to perform good karmas (actions). When you do not perform good karmas, you write a bad destiny for yourself. When that destiny hits you, your nature reacts negatively and you further perform bad Karmas. More bad karmas write bad destiny and when you hit that bad destiny, your nature again reacts badly. So one starts sinking and sinking till he hits into the life of lower worlds of insects and animals. Again, this is a journey but towards lower worlds.

When you have a mixed nature – good and bad. Your karmas are good and bad. Good karmas lead to good destiny and bad karmas lead to bad destiny. When the good destiny hits us, we enjoy pleasures and when the bad destiny hits us, we react and perform bad karmas. Person ascends to heaven to reap results of good karmas and suffers on earth due to bad karmas and also enjoys deeds on earth for the good karmas. So one is caught in the journey to heaven, re-birth, power, happiness, sufferings, material richness, old age, birth and death. Journey revolves around human birth cycles.

When Nature is very good, Karmas are good and you write a good destiny. A good destiny influences and gives opportunity to the pure hearted people to further perform good karmas. They do not hit bad destiny but there are certain mistakes that one will do out of ignorance. Karmas are karmas and do not recognize the ignorance part, so the only way to defeat the results of karmas is dispassion – leaving everything to Him, seeing Him as the doer and not yourself. Then He owns your Karmas and when He owns your Karmas, then you are on a journey to His home.

Now how do all these changes happen for the people in all the above vicious circles—it is meditation that makes the difference. Meditation brings purification and purification does wonders. Once nature is purified, then karmas are purified. Likewise, if karmas are purified, then nature is purified. Purification comes in from anywhere, whatever means, it will do wonders. Meditation is the most effective way to bring in the change, this is natural because we are talking of spiritual journey and meditation is taking help from the Lord whom we want to reach. It is taking help from the destination to pull us in the right direction. A person in sincere meditation will not go wrong.

'He whose mind remains unattached to sense-objects, derives through meditation, the Sattvika joy which dwells in the mind; then that Yogi, having completely identified himself through meditation with Brahma, enjoys eternal bliss'

— **Lord Krishna**

Bhagavad Gita, Chapter 6 Verse 21

Meditation is a way of identification with Him. Meditation brings eternal happiness that happiness once enjoyed is found by yogis to be much different from the happiness derived from material things. Who has tasted that happiness? See the yogis meditating in the Himalayas, away from the world. What do they have? They live in jungles, they do not get regular food and survive on some natural food and sometimes they do not even get that. They do not have permanent shelters and they tolerate the hardships of the weather and surroundings; they are away from their near and dear ones; they do not earn; they are unable to get regular clothes. What keeps them there? It is sheer bliss in meditation. These people can reveal what actual happiness means.

Now Lord Krishna advised KarmaYoga as superior to *Sankhyayoga* which means that one practicing Karmayoga does not need to leave anything but has to perform his natural duties with no expectations and by staying focused on God. This person derives the same happiness living among everyone, living in cities, having a family and money but the difference in this person is that he is in dispassion.

Way of his journey

The first one has adopted a different way of journey—it worked for him and this journey works for you living in a home life. Destination is same that is where Lord Krishna said that while two people have adopted a different journey, the real knowledge lies in the fact that the destination is same for both. Now they adopted different journeys due to their different nature.

However, *Bhagavad Gita* has advocated Karma yoga as superior to Sankhyayoga only from the point of view that it is easier to practice. The other one is difficult but the destination is same. The other one has much higher sacrifice and has lots of hardships compared to the one faced by KarmaYogi.

KarmaYogi has a different set of challenges. They are influenced and pulled in all directions. There is a possibility of going wrong.

There is no one in between you and Him. Guru guides you to His path. *Bhagavad Gita* guides you on the path to His home but if you see everyone is directly connected with Him. There is no one in-between. You worship Him, you do not worship Him through someone nor does He advise you to worship Him through someone. So, when there is no one between you and Him, you can decide on how to reach Him. So a saint said that the number of paths in which you can reach Him is the same as the number of Human Beings. Everyone can carve out his path to reach Him. That path will become clear through mediation. His path starts from where you are standing, you do not need to follow anyone, first you need to understand yourself and this understanding will have you decide the path on which you can reach Him.

'Among the great seers, I am Bhrgu; among words, I am the sacred syllable OM; among sacrifices, I am the sacrifice of Japa (muttering of sacred formulas); and among the immovables, the Himalayas.'

— **Lord Krishna**

Bhagavad Gita, Chapter 10 Verse 25

Sacrifice means that you do something for others—could be your children, society, poor, or deserving.

Lord says that among Sacrifices, I am *Japa* which means meditation or chanting Holy name. Meditation means that you are identifying yourself with Him. It helps you in changing the direction of your journey towards His home.

Meditation does multiple things starting with purification. When purification happens, you cannot go wrong in performing righteous karmas. With meditation, the light starts coming from inside. You start getting a natural feeling on what is right and what is not in the spiritual path even without referring to scriptures. Meditation will not let you go wrong. Also meditation helps reduce the impact of destiny where destiny was to hurt someone badly. It will make the impact bearable and may also pardon. When you are on the righteous path, Sanskara or good actions performed in past births start supporting the individual further to advance the journey faster. With meditation, some of the hindrances are easily overcome because firstly your vision has changed and you do not see some sufferings or hindrances as sufferings and just accept these as His blessing. This stops you from doing any further wrong action when faced with a challenging situation. Secondly, the hindrances are easily overcome as His blessings are getting showered all the time.

Mediation or Japa or chanting His Holy name does everything.

Hare Krishna Hare Krishna, Krishna Krishna Hare Hare Hare Rama Hare Rama, Rama Rama Hare Hare

This is called Hare Krishna MahaMantra and is treated as a complete worship.

Chanting the Holy name does wonders. Devotees have seen the impact and they can share on how it changes the journey starting with complete purification of the individuals. A purified soul will never go on to a wrong path.

'On those ever united through meditation with Me and worshipping Me with love, I confer that Yoga of wisdom by which they come to Me. In order to bestow My compassion on them, I, dwelling in their hearts, dispel their darkness born of ignorance by the illumination lamp of knowledge"

— **Lord Krishna**

Bhagavad Gita, Chapter 10 Verse 10 &11

This becomes clearer from the above that Meditation helps as you become wise in the spiritual journey with His blessings that come with Meditation. Meditation helps acquire the right knowledge and we had seen the power of knowledge. Right knowledge comes in the spiritual journey with Meditation.

Here Lord has also mentioned that He is dwelling in their hearts and He dispels their darkness born of ignorance. So with Meditation, the knowledge starts pouring from Inside as Lord is sitting inside everyone in the form of a soul. When you meditate with love, he blesses with the Yoga of wisdom. Wisdom means spiritual wisdom, wisdom to perform the righteous Karmas to reach His home within this birth.

Love does wonders if the love is spiritual love. A housewife can love her child as her child or can see Krishna in her child as a child is also His representation. This will naturally happen as the purification advances that you will see Him in everyone.

When a mother sees Him in the child, the love becomes eternal love, it becomes selfless love, it brings in humbleness and sacrifice and this awakened and advanced feeling of humbleness and sacrifice is the spiritual journey.

When you do not see a beggar as beggar but see him as a human who is also His creation but is going through the sufferings, then your offerings to that human being becomes spiritual. He is present everywhere, it is matter of us missing to see Him. He is present in flowers and fruits. His shine is present in Sun and Moon. He is there in the Air, nothing exists without Him. It is matter of a spiritual mind and spiritual eye that is needed to see Him in everything. He is never away from you. He is inside you. He is there all around you, we only miss to see Him. As a saint has said that whatever you see and wherever you see, you see Him only. It is a matter of recognition that we miss recognizing Him.

He does not miss to show His presence to us all the time. Meditation is also a journey and this is the most beautiful journey and this journey when advanced will show that He is everywhere and this journey ends at His home.

'Among the Vedic hymns, I am the hymn known as Gayatri'.

— **Lord Krishna**

Bhagavad Gita, Chapter 10 Verse 35

As we saw Hare Krishna Mantra above, *Gayatri Mantra* is also a Mahamantra. Mahamantra means complete worship.

When Hindu priests are born, they are taught by their elders that they need to chant Gayatri Mantra 2.4 million times during their lifetime. So, they regularly chant Gayatri Mantra. Gayatri Mantra is dedicated to Goddess Gayatri and Lord Krishna has also identified Himself as Gayatri Mantra in the hymns that are sung by eternally wise advancing their journey towards Him.

Gayatri Mantra is as follows:

"ॐ भूर्भुवः स्वः
तत्सवितुर्वरेण्यं
भर्गो देवस्य धीमहि
धियो योनः प्रचोदयात्।"

The meaning of the Gayatri mantra:

We contemplate the glory of Light illuminating the three worlds: gross, subtle, and causal. I am that supreme power, love, radiant illumination, and divine grace of universal intelligence. We pray for the divine light to illumine our minds.

Arya Samaj was found by Swami Dayanand. Worshippers in Arya Samaj chant Gayatri Mantra regularly during their morning, afternoon and evening prayers. They have placed Gayatri Mantra as above all the Mantras.

'Knowledge is better than practice without discernment, meditation on God is superior to knowledge, and renunciation of the fruit of actions is even superior to meditation; for, peace immediately follows renunciation.'

— **Lord Krishna**

Bhagavad Gita, Chapter 12 Verse 12

This verse has a very deep message. Firstly we all understand the importance of right knowledge. Right knowledge is needed to advance journey in the right direction. Without knowledge, you will not know where we are headed. Now Lord says, Meditation is superior to knowledge which means Meditation has the power to bring in the right knowledge. It purifies and hence the flow of right knowledge happens with it. Many housewives in the southern part of India are highly devoted to meditation without indulging into reading of spiritual texts frequently. Through meditation they derive the right knowledge and you find them performing their Natural Duties so well that is unfound in many others who are instead devoted to reading the scriptures or debating what is right and what is not. Just pure meditation and performing all Natural duties is enough to take you to His home.

Now comes the renunciation, when we read *Bhagavad Gita*, we find that Renunciation has been placed above everything. This is a must before one is able to reach His home. So *Bhagavad Gita* advises Sattvika Karmas as putting the journey in the right direction with Renunciation as a way to reach His home. Sattvika karmas alone take one to Heaven where one reaps the fruits of his meritorious deeds and returns to Human birth in a rich and pious family but the journey does not get rid of the birth and death cycles.

Renunciation is seeing oneself as the non-doer and seeing Him in everything that happens and leave everything to Him. This way you do not get to reap the fruits of righteous actions and defeat the way to Heaven and reach His home. But there seems to be one catch in this verse—can renunciation come in without chanting His holy name? So while renunciation is the highest state, that state can be reached only with Meditation and by chanting His holy name.

Renunciation and Dispassion

If you follow God or Devtas (blessed by God to fulfil the wishes of the individuals) for material gains, you go successful as the spiritual system responds to fulfil the wishes when followed sincerely with defined rituals.

The enlightened souls do not follow God's system for material gains but follow it for gaining God. Examples are Meera or Vrinda (Tulsi) or Gopis or Prahlad who had no desire other than attaining God. They were rich and could have enjoyed all the material gains but they realized that there is no gain like getting closer to God. Meera was a princess and then a queen. We read about her life and sacrifice to attain God and she reached Him.

So, God's promise to those souls was that whatever way you seek Me, I will respond accordingly as you are following His defined path in anyway.

Here is another story about the Gopis who loved Lord Krishna from their heart and had no other desire but to see Him all the time. Now how is this love different from the deep knowledge of scriptures?

There's a beautiful story from Sukhsagar. Udho was very close to Lord Krishna and was very knowledgeable about God's Home. So knowledge lets you know how God's Home looks like but does not necessarily mean that you will reach there. He was great worshipper of '*OM*'. Lord Krishna has identified Himself as OM as a God with no shape and called nirguana brahma.

Udho always worshipped OM. Lord Krishna has mentioned in *Bhagavad Gita* that identification with Nirguna (OM) comes with difficulty whereas one who is focused on Saguna (Lord Krishna) can get the identification more easily. There is no difference between the two. In fact they are similar, and it's just a matter of identification.

Lord Krishna loved Udho so he wanted to teach him the lessons of love and how it is different from the lessons of identification with Nirguna while the destination is again the same. Lord asked Udho to help impart his beautiful knowledge to Gopis who had no understanding of the eternal knowledge. But since they loved Him a lot, He asked Udho to go to Vrindavan and impart this knowledge to them. Udho accepted this task happily as it was a direction from Lord Krishna and he was undertaking a spiritual task. Lord Krishna gave him a letter addressed to Gopis and asked him to deliver the letter to Gopis.

When Udho reached Vrindavan, Gopis got very excited thinking that their Krishna (they called Him Kanhaiya) had also come but were disappointed to know that Kanhaiya had not come. But when Udho told them that he has brought a letter written by Lord Krishna addressed to them, they pounced on Him and in no time the letter got torn into hundreds of pieces with every Gopi holding a piece of the letter but no one was able to read what was written. To Udho's surprise , there was no regret also that letter has been torn to pieces. He felt that imparting knowledge to these Gopis was not going to be easy but then Lord Krishna had given Him this task so he had to perform it.

So, he told the Gopis that in case they did not know how to read the letter, they could have at least asked Udho to read it for them. Now no one knew what the message was. To his further surprise, there was no regret again. They were just happy that they had a piece of paper each or a leaf that was touched by Lord Krishna.

So, Udho started imparting the knowledge to Gopis but he found that they were so immersed in love with Lord Krishna, that they neither understood what he was talking about nor they wanted to make an attempt to understand. This was crafted by Lord Krishna to teach Udho what love means. He was full of tears when he returned from Vrindavan and met Lord Krishna. He told him that all along he had so much of pride that he was the one who had all the eternal knowledge but the real eternal knowledge was with Gopis, who knew nothing else but to love Him. He was completely transformed. Lord told Udho that he loved Udho so he wanted to break his pride and impart Him the real knowledge through which he would reach Lord Krishna.

See the heights of love that the Gopis had attained. No material benefit could lure them. Lord could not give them anything less than He himself as they had no other desire.

That is the real desire. So Lord has to give them return for their devotion, hence howsoever men seek Him he does respond to them. If you worship Him with no desire other than He himself, then He will come to you. If you worship him with desire for a material thing, then that material thing will come to you. Material thing will be with you till the end of the journey of this body, He will be with you above Time – always. Where do we want to settle?

'Karmayogi, who keeps his mind fixed on God, reaches Brahma in no time, Arjuna'

— **Lord Krishna**

Bhagavad Gita, Chapter 6 Verse 6

This is a beautiful message that a Karmayogi who is performing all his natural duties with dispassion and has fixed his mind on God reaches Brahma in no time. It is a short and fast journey to His home. Time is limited, things must change today and now. Journey must get set towards His home. He is there. Towards the end of *Bhagavad Gita* Lord Krishna had told Arjuna that having understood this yoga, you should not waste any time when you are not progressing towards Him. Lord said 'If you do not listen to me, you will be lost,' so what he meant was that you will be lost from the spiritual journey.

Once we lose the sight of this journey after having understood this journey, we do not know when we will get the opportunity to continue this journey again, so one should waste no time and no opportunity when we are not remembering Him.

Arjuna, there is no fall for him either here or hereafter. For, O My beloved, none who strives for self-redemption (i.e God realization) ever meets with evil destiny.

— **Lord Krishna**

Bhagavad Gita, Chapter 6 Verse 40

When the Journey Continues

A natural question comes to one's mind that if we go on to His path and we meet death before we could complete the journey, then what happens to us.

The same question came to Arjuna's mind in a different manner where he felt that the path defined for God's Home needs complete control on Mind and he felt that Mind is difficult to control like wind. That is where the question to this answer lies. One may not be able to exercise complete control in one birth unless one is committed to it. But the journey covered in one birth in direction of God's Home helps start the journey in next birth with a stronger foundation. But still Lord's spiritual advise to Arjuna was that having understood this secret, one should not waste time and try get to His home within this birth.

Next set of verses are a beautiful compilation in *Bhagavad Gita*, it really unfolds the key secrets which are not easily found elsewhere but they come out so clearly here. Also see the differences in the higher worlds and God's Home.

One does not meet with evil destiny when he strives for self-redemption. Here based on one's commitment, environment and struggle, one may not be able to complete the journey in one birth but the one who embarks on His path cannot meet with an evil destiny.

Such a person who has strayed from Yoga, obtains the higher worlds, (heaven etc.) to which men of meritorious deeds alone are entitled, and having resided there for innumerable years, takes birth of pious and prosperous parents.

— **Lord Krishna**

Bhagavad Gita, Chapter 6 Verse 41

Now the person who has strayed from Yoga meets with a good destiny. Firstly he enjoys the Higher Worlds for innumerable number of years (Now as we explained earlier the Time scale is very different in Higher Worlds and on earth. So earth equivalent, it may be even much higher number of years). Then he takes birth of pious and prosperous parents. So he does not need to go through the harshness of living environment and can continue his journey towards God's Home from where he left earlier. Here it again connects with our first chapter on 'Blessings by Birth'. These people are blessed by birth. So if you are blessed by birth, you can connect with your past births that it is result of meritorious deeds that you got these blessings else these would not have come. Now among the blessed people, some are very pious and continuing advancement of their journey to God's Home and some decide to move away from that journey and start moving towards material worlds.

Sanskara of past births will drive you to advance on the journey to God's home so that attraction will be there by birth but the material attraction is so strong that one can lose his path if one does not stay conscious. Maya (Material attraction) is also His creation so you need His blessings to overcome the pull of His Maya. This maya is Mahamaya, which is expansion of Yogamaya that we covered in the chapter of Yogamaya.

Or if he is possessed of dispassion, then not attaining to those regions he is born in the family of enlightened Yogis; but such a birth in this world is very difficult to obtain.

— **Lord Krishna**

Bhagavad Gita, Chapter 6 Verse 42

Now see how this person (above) in God's eyes is viewed so different from the earlier one. Both are pious, both meet with good destiny, both are considered to have done meritorious deeds but this one is possessed of Dispassion. Now when a person performing all his natural duties is also possessed of dispassion, he is entitled to continue his journey to God's Home immediately again.

Now see how God is extending a different kind of help to this person who is possessed of dispassion. God is allowing this person to bypass Heaven and he is re-born immediately in the family of enlightened Yogis. So, he continues his journey towards God's home with no break. The other one goes to Heaven and spends uncountable number of years in Heaven enjoying the results of meritorious deeds because this person has not been able to overcome his desires and to fulfil his desires, he is gifted with enjoyments in Heaven and in process he exhausts the merits of his good deeds and is re-born in the family of rich and pious. But this person by the time, he is re-born, has spent many years in heaven and has become poorer and since he is not yet away from desires, he carries a risk of attraction increasing towards material things when he is re-born while the attraction towards God will also be there by birth as that is carried by the individual soul.

However Yogi in dispassion who is rid of desires is born in the family of the enlightened Yogis and gifted with the right environment, has attraction towards God by birth, and works harder to finish the rest of his journey within the next birth. Now this birth comes rarely to some souls.

Firstly one of the thousands gets the opportunity to listen to Science of this soul. From those a rare one adopts that path. One who adopts that path is a deserving person in God's eyes. He is called an *Adhikari*.

Now when these rare people start their journey towards God, again rare examples get into dispassion. All of them get blessed but most of them get caught by Maya which is His creation and get into that circle.

Rare souls do not stop with the blessings showered and want to go to His home adopting dispassion and love for Him, embarking the real journey to His home.

Arjuna, he automatically regains in that birth the latencies of even-mindedness of his previous birth; and through that he strives harder than ever for perfection in the form of God –realization.

— **Lord Krishna**

Bhagavad Gita, Chapter 6 Verse 43

The other one who takes birth in a rich family, though under the sway of his senses, feels drawn towards God by force of the habit acquired in his previous birth; may, even the seeker of Yoga (in the form of even-mindedness) transcends the fruit of actions performed with some interested motive as laid down in the Vedas.

— **Lord Krishna**

Bhagavad Gita, Chapter 6 Verse 44

Both the births are good but people who have sensitivity of Time and understand what His home means will appreciate the immediate rebirth in the family of enlightened Yogis. Lord had mentioned earlier that those seeking to go to God's home will not follow that part of the Vedas where they are gifted with Heaven after the death and power with rebirth.

The Yogi, however, who diligently takes up the practice, attains perfection in this very life with the help of latencies of many births, and being thoroughly purged of sin, forthwith reaches the supreme state.

— Lord Krishna

Bhagavad Gita, Chapter 6 Verse 45

Now the message becomes more beautiful. This one is for those who practiced Dispassion. They practiced dispassion diligently and tried to get to perfection within this birth. Now in an effort to get to perfection, you will be faced with hardships and hindrances. These hindrances are nothing but latencies of past karmas and beautifully called as Destiny. But to overcome the hindrances due to past karmas, the help also comes from latencies of many births (of past karmas) and they help in overcoming the hindrances.

The message is imparted in a way simple, if the efforts are going on for God-realization, then latencies of past good karmas get amplified and come in support and latencies due to bad karmas of past births become weaker so that person can overcome these hindrances. Moving on to the path, he becomes purged of sin and reaches the supreme state.

The Yogi is superior to the ascetics; he is regarded superior even to those versed in sacred lore. The Yogi is also superior to those who perform action with some interested motive. Therefore, Arjuna do become a Yogi.

— **Lord Krishna**

Bhagavad Gita, Chapter 6 Verse 46

You do not need to leave home to get to dispassion. You need to get into dispassion performing all your natural duties like King Janaka who lived the life of a king, performed all duties of a king and was possessed of dispassion.

Of all the Yogis, again, he who devoutly worships Me with his mind focused on Me is considered by Me to be the best Yogi.

— **Lord Krishna**

Bhagavad Gita, Chapter 6 Verse 47

We have the inspiration to be the best yogi by worshipping Him all the time. We wish the readers a great journey to His home as the destination.

'That supreme Brahma is said to be the light of all lights and entirely beyond Maya. That godhead is knowledge itself, worth knowing, and worth attaining through real wisdom, and is particularly abiding in the hearts of all.'

— **Lord Krishna**

Bhagavad Gita, Chapter 13 Verse 17

He is worth attaining through real wisdom. He is beyond Maya and is abiding in the hearts of all.

'Neither the sun nor the moon nor fire can illumine that supreme self –effulgent state, attaining which they never return to this world; that is my supreme abode'

— **Lord Krishna**

Bhagavad Gita, Chapter 15 Verse 6

'Resigning all your duties to Me, The all-powerful and all supporting Lord, take refuge in Me alone; I shall absolve you of all sins, worry not'

— **Lord Krishna**

Bhagavad Gita, Chapter 18 Verse 66

Complete Surrender

God is known to be unconquerable, but one who submissively hears the words of a self-realized soul conquers the unconquerable.

Srimad-Bhagavatam 4.24.53,
Srila Prabhupada

Lord Krishna had shown the end of the war to Arjuna when Arjuna wanted to see the 'Virata Swarup' of Lord Krishna, in which Lord had shown that all the Principle warriors in both the armies are going to die. Arjuna had known the end of the war even before the war started. Not only he had known the end of the war, he had seen the end of the war with his own eyes.

'I am mighty Kala (the eternal Time-spirit), the destroyer of the worlds. I am out to exterminate these people. Even without you all those warriors, arrayed in the enemy's camp shall die.'

— **Lord Krishna**

Bhagavad Gita, Chapter 11 Verse 32

So Lord Krishna told Arjuna that irrespective of whether Arjuna fights this war or not, all these people will die because Lord is at this time 'Mahakaal' and these people must die.

Lord Krishna showed a very different relationship between God and Humans. This was never seen before. He drove the chariot of Arjuna. He ate with all the families. He slept with His cousins and brothers, counselled everyone, including Dhritrashtra and Duryodhana, many times on how this war can be avoided. He even went with a proposal to give five villages to the five Pandava brothers so that they could live their life. Kaurvas dismissed all other doors and opened the door to the battlefield.

When Arjuna saw the *virata* form and understood that Krishna with whom he has been living all his life is indeed the Supreme Lord, he was highly moved.

'Lord, prostrating my body at Your feet and bowing low I seek to propitiate You, the ruler of all and worthy of all praise, It behoves You to bear with me even as a father bears with his son, a friend with his friend and a husband with his beloved spouse'

— **Arjuna**

Bhagavad Gita, Chapter 11 Verse 44

Arjuna proposed a very different relationship with God. This is what makes a difference that God can be with you in any and every form. He is not situated in another universe where your voice may not get heard nor is he expecting you to keep a distance and bow down with shivers.

'With your mind thus devoted to Me, you shall, by My grace overcome all difficulties. But, if from self-conceit you do not care to listen to Me, you will be lost'

— **Lord Krishna**

Bhagavad Gita, Chapter 18 Verse 58

'If taking your stand on egotism, you think I will not fight', vain is this resolve of yours; nature will drive you to the act.

— **Lord Krishna**

Bhagavad Gita, Chapter 18 Verse 59

Lord Krishna is further saying to Arjuna that he will not be able to decide against the war because his nature is that of a warrior. This shows the influence of the nature on an individual. While Arjuna was an enlightened person, he was a born warrior and this war was for protection of the right. Lord said that Nature will drive you to this act.

That action, too, which you are not willing to undertake through ignorance you will perforce perform, bound by own duty borne of your nature.

— **Lord Krishna**

Bhagavad Gita, Chapter 18 Verse 60

Lord further affirms that Arjuna has taken a decision of not going into the war out of ignorance but such is the influence of Nature and Natural duty that it will force him into the war.

O Arjuna, God abides in the heart of all creatures, causing them to revolve according to their Karma by His illusive power (Maya) as though mounted on a machine.

— **Lord Krishna**

Bhagavad Gita, Chapter 18 Verse 61

Lord further said that if for the reasons of attachment, he still takes a decision not to fight, that decision will not work as God sitting inside him will take over and drive him into the war governed and guided by his previous Karmas. The reason God will take over is because destiny has decided this war to happen this way.

Now we see the messages from Lord that how Karmas, Nature and Destiny are so interwoven. Not only they are interwoven but they are getting strictly governed by God as

God is saying that Nature is revolving the individuals as if mounted on a machine according to their Karmas.

Now Arjuna is in the middle of the battlefield with a number of thoughts in his head. War is about to begin. He has his relatives on the opposite side. He has Lord Himself driving his chariot. Krishna has just revealed to him that he is Lord. Krishna and has also reminded him that he is a warrior and he must fight the righteous unsolicited war. He has also seen the end of the war. Krishna has also told him that he has no choice but to fight as destiny is already written and God sitting inside him will drive him into the war.

In such a situation, Lord goes further to tell him that what he should do and that is the message for all the devotees and that is what takes a devotee to Lord's home.

'Take refuge in Him alone with all your being, Arjuna. By His mere grace you will attain supreme peace and the eternal abode'

— **Lord Krishna**

Bhagavad Gita, Chapter 18 Verse 62

Hence God is asking Arjuna to come to His shelter. God is promising that He will absolve him of all sins and take Him to His abode. Now only the Supreme Power can pardon all the sins, no one else has the power to absolve him of all the sins.

'Resigning all your duties to Me, The all-powerful and all-supporting Lord, take refuge in Me alone; I shall absolve you of all sins, worry not'

— **Lord Krishna**

Bhagavad Gita, Chapter 18 Verse 66

Lord is asking Arjuna to come to His shelter and offer all his duties to the Lord and in turn Lord is promising Arjuna that He will pardon him of all the sins that he has performed in the past. Once rid of sins, he will reach His abode.

Hence the message for the devotees is that He is the one who can pardon the sins that may have been knowingly or unknowingly committed in the last many births. Only an ultimate can pardon the sins and take one to His home, above Time.

Wishing all readers a great Journey to the Supreme

Other books by same authors

Secrets of Living
Rajiv Sachdev & Neeraj Gupta
978 81 207 6658 7

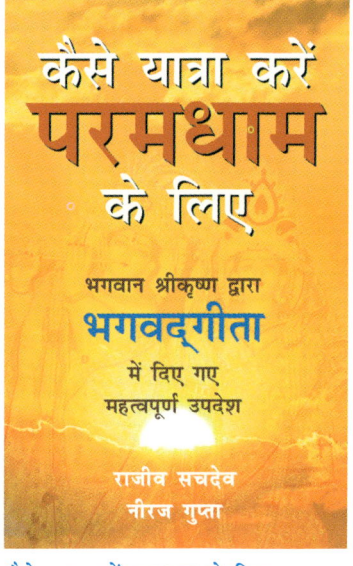

कैसे यात्रा करें परमधाम के लिए
राजीव सचदेव एवं नीरज गुप्ता
978 81 207 8318 3

ebook can be downloaded through amazon and other ebook distributors